KeyWords to Nail Your Job Interview

By Wendy S. Enelow

100 Winning Cover Letters for $100,000+ Jobs

100 Winning Resumes for $100,000+ Jobs

101 Ways to Recession-Proof Your Career

1500+ Keywords for $100,000+ Jobs

Best KeyWords for Resumes, Covers Letters, and Interviews

Best Cover Letters for $100,000+ Jobs

Best Resumes and CVs for International Jobs

Best Resumes for $100,000+ Jobs

Best Resumes for People Without a Four-Year Degree

Cover Letter Magic

Expert Resumes for Computer and Web Jobs

Expert Resumes for Managers and Executives

Expert Resumes for Manufacturing Careers

Expert Resumes for People Returning to Work

Expert Resumes for Teachers and Educators

KeyWords to Nail Your Job Interview

Resume Winners From the Pros

Winning Interviews for $100,000+ Jobs

THE AUTHOR: Wendy S. Enelow is a recognized leader in the executive job search, career coaching and resume writing industries. In private practice for 20 years, she has assisted thousands of job search candidates through successful career transitions. She is now the Founder and President of the Career Masters Institute, an exclusive training and development association for career professionals worldwide. A graduate of the University of Maryland, Wendy has earned several distinguished professional credentials - Certified Professional Resume Writer (CPRW), Job and Career Transition Coach (JCTC), and Credentialed Career Master (CCM). Wendy can be contacted at wendyenelow@cminstitute.com.

Keywords *to* Nail *Your* Job Interview

WENDY S. ENELOW, CPRW, JCTC, CCM

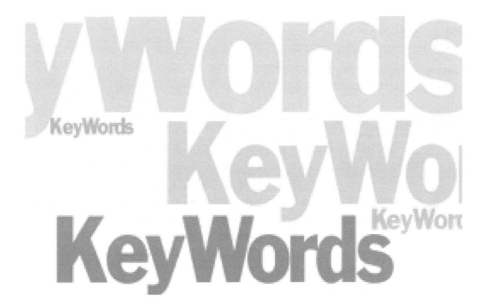

IMPACT PUBLICATIONS
MANASSAS PARK, VIRGINIA

ISBN: 1-57023-212-1

Library of Congress: 2004100256

Publisher: For information on Impact Publications, including current and forthcoming publications, authors, press kits, online bookstore, and submission requirements, visit the left navigation bar on the front page of our main company website: www.impactpublications.com.

Publicity/Rights: For information on publicity, author interviews, and subsidiary rights, contact the Media Relations Department: Tel. 703-361-7300, Fax 703-335-9486, or email: info@impactpublications.com.

Sales/Distribution: All bookstore sales are handled through Impact's trade distributor: National Book Network, 15200 NBN Way, Blue Ridge Summit, PA 17214, Tel. 1-800-462-6420. All special sales and distribution inquiries should be directed to the publisher: Sales Department, IMPACT PUBLICATIONS, 9104 Manassas Drive, Suite N, Manassas Park, VA 20111-5211, Tel. 703-361-7300, Fax 703-335-9486, or email: info@impactpublications.com.

Contents

KeyWords to Nail Your Job Interview

Chapter 1

Using KeyWords
in Your Job Search

What Are KeyWords?

Before we begin any discussion of KeyWord Interviewing, it is essential that we first discuss KeyWords – what they are, where they came from, and how they pertain to each individual job seeker and his/her specific job search. And, as always, the best place to start with a new concept is with a clear definition:

> *KeyWord: The "hot" words associated with a specific industry, profession, or job function…generally a noun, short phrase, abbreviation, or acronym. When used effectively, a KeyWord or KeyWord phrase can communicate an entire message with just a simple word or two.*

Ten years ago no one had ever heard of KeyWords, yet alone KeyWord Resumes, KeyWord Scanning, or KeyWord-Based Interviewing. Today, however, the concept of KeyWords is everywhere you look and a vital component for every job seeker's success. Consider this:

- You talk to a resume writer, recruiter, career coach, career counselor, outplacement consultant, or human resources professional, and each of them stresses the importance of KeyWords in today's competitive job search market.

- You read an article on the latest employment trends and the focus of the article is on the Internet and KeyWord Scanning as a method for identifying potential hires with the *right* skills and qualifications.

- You attend a job search training seminar and the facilitator stresses how critical KeyWords are when writing a great resume and *nailing* your interviews.

- You listen to a CNN news broadcast about the latest employment trends and the reporter highlights the importance of KeyWords in today's electronic job search market.

- You purchase a book on resume writing, cover letter writing, job search, or interviewing, and the focus of each book is on KeyWords and how vital they are to your successful job search campaign.

- You search the Internet for job leads and postings, and virtually every ad instructs you to include the appropriate KeyWords in your resume, cover letter, and other job search communications.

- You consult with an interview coach and she stresses the importance of KeyWords in crafting powerful responses to each and every interview question.

Yet, KeyWords are nothing new. In fact, you've probably used many of them throughout your working life. They are buzz words – the "hot" words associated with a specific industry, profession, or job function – that clearly communicate a specific message about a specific job function, qualification, accomplishment, or responsibility. KeyWord examples include employee relations (*for Human Resource professionals*), new product launch (*for Marketing professionals*), contract negotiations (*for Sales professionals*), distribution management (for *Transportation professionals*), ISO 14000 (*for Manufacturing professionals*), and network design (*for Information Technology professionals*).

Today, trends in resume writing, interviewing, hiring, and employment have changed, greatly influenced by the tremendous competition in the job search market and the recent difficult economic times. To be effective in your job search and catch an employer's interest, resumes, cover letters, and your responses to interview questions must be action-driven and clearly demonstrate the value you bring to a company. And there is no better manner in which to accomplish this than with the use of powerful KeyWords and KeyWord phrases that showcase your qualifications, capabilities, and skills.

KeyWords for Specific Industries & Professions

To help you understand the concept of KeyWords and their powerful use, here is a sample listing of KeyWords and KeyWord Phrases for the 16 industries and professions in Chapters 4 through 19 of this book, and the specific message that each communicates.

Industry/Profession	Keyword/KeyWord Phrase	Message It Communicates
Accounting & Finance	Financial Analysis	Competency in financial data collection, analysis, reporting, and recommendations
Banking & Investment	Private Banking	Competency in customer relationship management, banking products and services, sales, and financial advisory services
Customer Service	Customer Loyalty	Competency in developing, managing, and retaining customer accounts and customer relationships
Education	Curriculum Development	Competency in identifying learner needs and creating educational programs and instructional materials to meet those needs
Engineering	New Product Design	Competency in the design, development, engineering, and prototyping of new products and new technologies
Health Care	Discharge Planning	Competency in preparing patients for discharge, educating patients and caregivers, and coordinating resources between various health care practitioners
Hospitality	Labor Cost Controls	Competency in capturing cost savings by realigning and better utilizing staff resources
Human Resources	Benefits Administration	Competency in the selection, administration, and management of employee benefit programs
Human Services	Crisis Intervention	Competency in effectively responding to crisis situations and deploying the appropriate personnel and resources
International Business	Joint Venture	Competency in identifying opportunities and then structuring and negotiating joint venture transations
Legal	Discovery	Competency in legal research, data, and document collection, and legal analysis
Manufacturing	Quality Assurance	Competency in identifying quality deficiencies and implementing systems, processes, and technologies to enhance the quality of operations, documents, and products.

Retail	Merchandising	Competency in product selection, display, and promotion
Sales & Marketing	Territory Management	Competency in the management of products, personnel, services, and/or customer relationships within a defined region
Senior & Executive Management	Profit/Loss Management	Competency in financial management to ensure company profitability
Technology	Database Administration	Competency in the design, administration, and management of database technologies

Now, do you see the tremendous power that KeyWords have? By using just one or two short words, you can communicate a wealth of information about your specific skills, knowledge, and qualifications. KeyWords will give you the power that you need in order to nail each and every interview and *close the deal*.

One other important concept to consider in a general discussion of KeyWords is that a minor change to a KeyWord or KeyWord Phrase can significantly alter its meaning. Here's just one example:

KeyWord Phrase: Sales Negotiations
Message: Negotiate customer sales contracts, pricing, terms, and conditions.

KeyWord Phrase: Executive Negotiations
Message: Negotiate directly with top-level decision makers.

KeyWord Phrase: International Negotiations
Message: Negotiate with international customers, vendors, and suppliers.

"Professional" KeyWords

Now that I've outlined KeyWord samples for specific industries and professions, let's discuss more general, *professional* KeyWords that are equally important to communicate during your interviews and in your resume, cover letter, and other job search communications. Select the *professional* KeyWords from the list below that match your own experience and then be sure to use them throughout all phases of your job search.

- Business Planning
- Customer Service
- Performance & Productivity Improvement
- Business Process Design & Optimization

- P&L Management
- Project Management
- Change Management
- PC Technology
- Consensus Building
- International Business
- Efficiency Improvement
- Revenue Growth

- Team Building & Team Leadership
- Oral & Written Communications
- Problem Solving & Decision Making
- Presentations & Negotiations
- Organization & Administration
- PC & Internet Technology
- Cost Reduction & Avoidance
- Bottom-Line Profit Improvement

The potential list of your *professional* KeyWords goes on and on. See how many more you can think of, and use them to create sentences and phrases that will give your resumes, cover letters, and interviews an energy and power of their own.

My Own "Professional" KeyWord Toolkit:

_____

_____

_____

_____

_____

_____

Using KeyWords to Facilitate Your Career Change

Another excellent use of the KeyWords in this book is to educate yourself about the skills, qualifications, and knowledge required in professions other than your own. Suppose your entire career has been in the manufacturing industry and you're now interested in pursuing opportunities in sales and marketing. Carefully review the KeyWords for sales and marketing to better familiarize yourself with what is required of a qualified candidate, and compare them to your background to see what experiences you have that required those same skills. Then, incorporate those KeyWords into your job search materials and interview responses to demonstrate to a prospective employer that you have the *right* stuff.

Action Verbs

Just as KeyWords are an essential component of your job search and interviews, so are Action Verbs, words used to present your qualifications, achievements, and results (*your KeyWords*) in an action-driven style. Action Verbs are common verbs such as organized, delivered, led, negotiated, administered, transacted, designed, conceived, created, reengineered, and directed. These are the words that will give your resume and interview responses energy, power, and punch.

For example, suppose you want to use the KeyWord phrase *customer service*. In essence, you have two options:

When Action Verbs are NOT used:
Responsible for the daily operations of the customer service center.

When Action Verbs are used:
Planned, staffed, and managed the daily operations of a 45-employee customer service center.

It's obvious that the sentence using the Action Verbs comes across more powerfully and is a much better reflection of the quality and caliber of experience you might bring to a prospective employer. Refer to Chapter 20 for a detailed listing of Action Verbs, High-Impact Phrases, and Personality Descriptors that you can use in all of your interviews and job search communications.

About This Book

KeyWords to Nail Your Job Interview is the first book on the subject of KeyWord interviewing and is an essential tool to help you prepare for interviews and position yourself as the #1 candidate for each and every job opportunity. As you work your way through the text, here's what you'll find:

Chapter 1: Using KeyWords in Your Job Search

This introductory chapter provides valuable and informative reading about the importance of KeyWords and how to use them throughout all phases of your job search - resume writing, cover letter writing, and job interviews.

Chapter 2: KeyWords for Powerful Interviews

This chapter will demonstrate how you can write a KeyWord resume that will make your interviewer's job easier! By providing your interviewer with essential KeyWord information about your skills and qualifications, your interviewer will immediately focus on information that is important to the company and in which you have experience. It becomes a "win-win" for everyone!

Chapter 3: Strategies & Techniques for KeyWord-Based Interviewing

A detailed discussion of how to use KeyWords in your interviews to ensure that you quickly and accurately communicate the *right* information for each and every position for which you interview.

Chapters 4-19: KeyWord Interview Toolkits for 16 Industries & Professions

These chapters are the most important in this book! In them you'll find the top 10 KeyWords for 16 different industries and professions, each used in a mock interview Q&A to demonstrate how to translate those KeyWords into action and results. In addition, you'll also find a KeyWord accomplishment phrase for each that you can memorize and use in your interviews and/or incorporate into your resume and cover letter.

Chapter 20: Action Verbs, High-Impact Phrases, & Personality Descriptors

Here you'll find more than 500 Action Verbs, High-Impact Phrases, and Personality Descriptors that you can communicate during your interviews and use in your resume and cover letter. Review these lists carefully, select the words and phrases that accurately reflect your career, qualifications, and experience, and then incorporate them into all aspects of your search campaign. Just like KeyWords, they will give you power to perform well in any interview situation.

Which KeyWords are Right for Me?

No KeyWord list is comprehensive. Words, language, and communication are fluid and dynamic, and cannot be boiled down into something that is finite and limited. With that said, know that this book was written to provide you with a vast selection of KeyWords and KeyWord Phrases that you can use in your job search. However, just as important, you'll want to add other KeyWords that accurately reflect the additional skills and qualifications you offer to a prospective employer.

You already know the answer to that question! You've got the KeyWords in your hand if you're reading this book. As you review the KeyWords that are specific to your career, you'll see that many represent the functions you perform on a daily basis. Others may be new words to you, but I'm sure you're familiar with their underlying concepts. In fact, I'm sure most of these KeyWords reflect the skills and experience you've gained throughout your career.

Now that you've got a great KeyWord resource, use it to:

- Create powerful resumes, cover letters, thank-you letters, career profiles, and other job search communications. *Let prospective employers know that you've got the "right" skills and qualifications to meet their needs.*

- Communicate your skills, qualifications, and achievements during all of your job interviews. *Demonstrate that you have the "right" skills and you'll be well on your way to great job offers and wonderful new opportunities.*

Chapter 2

KeyWords for
Powerful Interviews

What is a KeyWord Resume?

Although this book is really about KeyWord-based interviewing, no book on KeyWords would be complete without a discussion of how to use KeyWords to your best advantage in both your resume and cover letter. We'll start with a discussion of KeyWord resumes first.

Today, KeyWords are a vital component of every job seeker's resume. As we discussed in Chapter 1, KeyWords are what give your resume power and communicate that you have the right skills and qualifications for the position you are seeking. Yet, how and where you include your KeyWords in your resume is entirely up to you as there are several options which are outlined below. You can make the decision about where to place your KeyWords based on a combination of the following:

How you can use your KeyWords to grab the attention of prospective employers.
How your KeyWords will fit comfortably within the text of your resume.
Visually, how you can best highlight your KeyWords based on the resume format that you've chosen.

It is important to note that this book is not about resume writing. Rather, this section of the book focuses on how best to integrate KeyWords into your resume. If you need a resource to help you write and design your own winning resume, I would recommend either of the following books:

Best Resumes for People Without a Four-Year Degree (Impact Publications, 2003)
Best Resumes for $100,000+ Jobs (Impact Publications, 2002)

Following are five strategies you can use to include KeyWords in your resume. We'll explore each of them.

1. **Include your KeyWords in a separate section,** either at the beginning or the end of your resume. You can title this section KeyWords, KeyWord Summary, Professional Qualifications, Professional Skills, Skills Summary, Skills Profile, Career Profile, or Technology Qualifications.

KEYWORDS:

Executive Secretary / Office Manager with 12 years' experience. Qualifications include:

*Executive & Board Relations	*Executive Office Management
*Regulatory Reporting	*Staff Training & Development
*Confidential Correspondence	*Federal Property Acquisition
*Special Events Planning	*Customer Relationship Management
& Management	

---

2. **Integrate your KeyWords into the summary** at the beginning of your resume to create a fluid paragraph that reads well, highlights your most notable skills (KeyWords), and communicates action and results. In this situation, what you're really doing is wrapping text around your KeyWords.

CAREER SUMMARY:

Highly experienced, client-oriented Software Development and Programming Manager. Accomplished leader, capable of building motivated and productive teams. Significant software design and engineering expertise. Project management responsibility for both government and industry projects, including RFP preparation, subcontractor negotiations, budgeting, and technical documentation. P&L management experience. MBA degree.

---

3. **Share KeyWord success stories in your resume** that you can expand on in the interview. If you know, for example, that a company is specifically interested in a candidate with a wealth of experience in retail merchandising, then be sure to highlight one, two, or even three examples of your specific merchandising projects and achievements. Success stories are best described in a resume with a 3-step approach: first, briefly explain the situation of the company, its goals or its challenges as they relate to merchandising; second, briefly

explain your action plan (what you did); and, finally, highlight your related achievements and success.

Regional Sales Manager (2001 to Present)
EXCELSIOR CONSUMER PRODUCTS, Tampa, FL

Challenge: Recruited by National Sales Director to revitalize the non-performing Tampa market and return the region to **profitability** after three years of consecutive losses.

Action: Hired and trained **field sales team**, launched several **new product lines**, restored failed **customer relationships**, and targeted new customers throughout the **emerging** technology and telecommunications markets.

Results: **Increased sales revenues** 215% and **restored profitability** within first year.
Captured 12 new **key accounts** generating an additional $3.5 million in annual sales.
Recruited and **trained** three new sales representatives promoted to **account management** positions.
Won the 2002 and 2003 **"Regional Sales Manager of the Year"** awards.

---

4. **Integrate your KeyWords into the job descriptions** in your resume. In fact, it would almost be impossible not to do this in a resume since your job descriptions are written to summarize and highlight your qualifications, and many of those qualifications are indeed the precise KeyWords that you want to communicate in your resume.

Controller (1999 to 2002)
AMES DISTRIBUTION, Detroit, MI

Recruited to join the **accounting** and **financial management** team of a professional services corporation. Challenged to strengthen **accounting practices**, streamline **financial reporting** processes, and improve the quality of **financial data**. Concurrently, managed corporate **legal**, **tax**, and **administrative** affairs. Led **investor presentations**, negotiated **corporate credit transactions**, and coordinated all **regulatory filings**.

---

5. **Use KeyWords to highlight your achievements** in your resume. Again, just as above, it is difficult not to use KeyWords in your achievement statements since your achievements reflect your skills and knowledge, which, in many instances, are your preferred KeyWords.

> **Health Care Administrator** (1998 to Present)
> UNION HEALTH CARE ASSOCIATES, Pittsburgh, PA
>
> *Project Highlights & Career Achievements:*
>
> - Led **health care practice** through successful transition to thrive in a **managed-care** environment.
> - Designed new market-driven, community-oriented **patient care model**.
> - Consultant for start-up **home pain management therapy program** that grew to $2.8 million in first-year **revenues**.
> - **Mentored** new physicians, helping to grow practice 30%.
> - Researched and implemented **computerized digital technology** for in-house medical testing and results reporting.
> - Spearheaded the introduction of leading-edge **quality care models** and systems.

It is critical to understand that you do not have to select only one of the five examples above. You may combine several of these strategies into various sections throughout your resume to create a true KeyWord resume.

One final note: As you'll notice above, I've highlighted all the KeyWords in bold print so that you can easily identify them. Most resumes will not have all the KeyWords in bold. This can, however, be a good strategy as long as you do not overdo the bold print. If you use too much bolding, nothing will stand out. If you want to highlight each KeyWord in your resume, but feel that the bold print is too much, you might consider using italics or underlining as your preferred type enhancement.

How Do I Use KeyWords in My Cover Letter?

KeyWords are also remarkably effective tools for use in developing your cover letters and broadcast letters (*letters sent without a resume; generally longer than the more typical cover letter*). They strengthen the presentation of your skills, qualifications, and experience, as well as demonstrate your competencies, achievements, and successes. What's more, you can, and should, customize your cover letters for each position for which you apply. Cover letters are always most effective when they highlight specific KeyWords that coincide with a specific employer's needs, hiring requirements, and objectives. For example, if an advertisement asks for a candidate with experience in supply chain management, be sure to include those specific words in your cover letter, along with purchasing, logistics, materials management, storeroom management, and any other related skills (KeyWords) that you offer.

As with your resume, KeyWords can be used in various cover letter sections, styles, and formats. Following are four cover letter excerpts to demonstrate how best to integrate KeyWords into your letters.

1. **Integrate your KeyWords into the text** of your cover letter. This is, by far, the most common approach for using KeyWords in cover letters.

   My career is best summarized as follows: Years of **senior management** experience with two **global** corporations - Excelsior Bank and Voice of America - and now my current position as **President/CEO** of a **start-up technology venture**. The breadth of my experience is remarkably broad, from managing VOA's entire **Latin American operation** to the more finite functions of building an **operating architecture** and **business infrastructure** for a new and highly specialized enterprise.

2. **Include your KeyWords in a separate skills section** in your cover letter. This strategy is the best to use if you want to draw immediate visual attention to your KeyWords.

   Highlights of my professional skills that most closely relate to your needs include the following:

* **Strategic Sales & Market Planning**	* **New Product Introduction**
* **Competitive Sales Negotiations**	* **Sales Training & Leadership**
* **Account Development & Management**	* **Client Retention & Loyalty**
* **Competitive Market Intelligence**	* **US & International Sales**
   ---

3. **Use your KeyWords to highlight your career achievements** in your cover letter. This strategy accomplishes two things at once by drawing immediate attention to both your achievements and your core skills.

   Highlights of my career that may be of particular interest to you include the following:

   - Ten years' experience as **Managing Director, Senior VP, Executive VP, COO**, and, now, **President/CEO**.

   - Success in **start-ups, acquisitions, turnarounds, high-growth companies**, and **multinational organizations**.

   - Innovative performance in **business development** through **internal growth, mergers, acquisitions, joint ventures**, and **strategic alliances**.

- Outstanding **P&L** performance measured via **revenue** and **profit growth**, **cost reduction**, **market penetration**, and other key indices.

- Expertise in **sales**, **marketing**, and the entire **customer development/ management** process.

4. Use your KeyWords to respond to specific job posting requirements. This is often referred to as the quick-and-dirty strategy as you are reiterating the employer's hiring criteria while simultaneously highlighting how you meet each and every one of those requirements.

Your Qualifications	My Experience
MBA Degree	**MBA** Degree from **Harvard Business School.**
Human Resources Management	10 years' experience in **HRM** and **OD**.
HRIS Technology	Implementation of $2.8 million **HRIS technology.**
Benefits & Compensation	Design of IBM's **compensation plans**.
Management Recruitment	**Recruitment** of IBM's newest executive team.

Again, as I mentioned in our discussion about resumes, this book is not about cover letter writing. If you need a resource to help you write and design your cover letters, I would recommend *Best Cover Letters for $100,000+ Jobs* (Impact Publications, 2002). Although all 100+ cover letter samples in the book are for candidates looking for jobs that pay $100,000 or more, the same concepts, strategies, and formats are applicable to every job seeker.

Where Else Can You Use Your KeyWords?

KeyWords are also powerful tools to incorporate into all of your other job search materials to be sure that you are communicating the specific skills, qualifications, and expertise that an employer is requesting. Consider integrating your KeyWords into:

- Leadership Profiles
- Career Biographies
- Thank-You Letters
- Internet Resume Postings
- Networking Letters
- Print Resume Portfolios
- Online Resume Portfolios

In fact, you can also use KeyWords in general business correspondence, proposals, reports, capital financing requests, advertisements, marketing communications, publicity, publications, and public speaking presentations. In each and every one of these situations, you are also trying to communicate that you have the right qualifications and skills. Let your KeyWords work for you - whether looking for a new job or in the course of doing your current job. The use of KeyWords in your professional documents is limited only by your imagination.

KeyWords and Scanning Technology

Before we leave our discussion of KeyWords and their importance in writing resumes, cover letters, and other job search communications, it is essential, in today's technology age, to highlight the importance of KeyWords to the resume scanning process.

In decades long since past, actual people read and reviewed resumes! Today, KeyWords are often the standard by which companies and recruiters screen applicants' resumes to identify core skills and qualifications. Using advanced KeyWord scanning technology, resumes are electronically reviewed to identify the KeyWords that match the specific hiring criteria. As such, it is critical that you include those KeyWords in your resume, cover letters, and all other job search communications. Whether this electronic strategy for evaluating a candidate's qualifications is an appropriate and effective tool or not, the fact remains that KeyWord scanning has become an increasingly dominant tool in today's hiring market.

It is important to note that KeyWords do not have to be in any particular section, or even in a separate section, on your resume or cover letter to get noticed. Scanning technology is evolving as quickly as other technologies and can easily identify a KeyWord no matter where it is positioned in a document.

Do not allow yourself to be passed over because you do not have the right words in your resume. Integrate the KeyWords from this book into your resume as they accurately reflect your experience. Not only will you meet the technological requirements for KeyWord scanning, you will also create powerful career marketing tools. And we all know that the winning job applicants are those who can sell their qualifications, highlight their achievements, and distinguish themselves from the competition. Let the KeyWords in this book help you do just that.

KeyWord Resumes, Cover Letters, and the Interview

The best place to start when discussing KeyWords and interviews is to ask yourself the following question:

> *How can an interviewer use my KeyWord resume and cover letter to better and more effectively interview me?*

The answer to that question is straightforward. When a prospective employer, recruiter, or human resources professional looks at a KeyWord resume or cover letter, it makes their job so much easier! By highlighting your core skills, competencies, achievements, and career experiences - in a manner that is easy to identify - all your interviewer needs to do is glance at your resume and cover letter and all your KeyWords pop right out. No more struggling through paragraphs of text to identify your key skills; no more frustration in trying to guess whether or not you have the right skills and experience for the job; no more difficulty in determining whether your skills match their needs. You've made it easy for them, and that instantly positions you as a candidate worth considering.

Now that the hiring manager's job is easier, what happens? Three important things:

1. The hiring manager can readily see your KeyWords and, in turn, your qualifications. Hopefully, you've researched the company, determined their specific needs and challenges, and highlighted the appropriate KeyWords in both your resume and cover letter.

2. The hiring manager can then use your KeyWords to ask you specific questions about your experience and those job functions as they relate to that company's needs. Rather than using a pre-scripted list of interview questions, your interviewer can customize your interview to the company's specific needs and your specific qualifications. This, in and of itself, will give you a decided advantage over any competition.

3. You put yourself in the advantageous position of a candidate to consider, since you've been so effective in highlighting your skills. Rather than ending up in the circular file, you're on top of the preferred pile. What a great place to be!

In the next chapter, we'll explore in detail the specific strategies and techniques for KeyWord-based interviewing, a new trend in behavioral-based interviewing, and the key to job search success in today's intensely competitive market.

Chapter 3

Strategies & Techniques for KeyWord-Based Interviewing

KeyWord-based interviewing is a new approach to job interviewing which combines the two well-established concepts of behavioral interviewing and KeyWord usage to create an entirely new methodology. Here's the equation:

> **Behavioral Interviewing**
> (*based on the belief that past behavior is the best predictor of future behavior*)
>
> +
>
> **KeyWords**
> (*the "hot" words associated with a specific industry, profession, or job function*)
>
> =
>
> **KeyWord-Based Interviewing**
> (*the use of KeyWords to demonstrate behavioral competencies*)

Now, let's explore each of these concepts individually.

Behavioral Interviewing

Behavioral interviewing emerged onto the employment scene in the 1990s as companies nationwide, and worldwide, began to look at their employees in a much different light. All of a sudden, companies were faced with downsizings, reorganizations, mergers, hostile takeovers, and more. The results of those radical changes and the impact they have had on companies worldwide have been the subject of hundreds, if not thousands, of books and articles over the past two decades. Our task here is not to examine, or even discuss, all of those changes. Our focus is on how those changes have impacted the way in which companies hire and why behavioral interviewing has become such a key component of the new hiring process.

As a result of the tremendous financial impact of these major corporate events, companies began to look at the true cost of their employees. When you consider the money involved in recruiting, interviewing, hiring, and training good employees, you're looking at an average of several thousand dollars per hire. As such, companies began to truly appreciate how costly it was to hire new people and how essential it is to retain those people.

The next obvious question to ask was how could they better ensure that their new employees would stay with the company. The longer the length of stay, the lower the actual cost of each new hire who remains as a productive and efficient employee. Essential to retaining these people were several key considerations that slowly, but surely, companies began to accept.

1. **Companies had to ensure that they hired people with the right skills for the jobs that were to be done.**
   If the prospective employee's past work behavior demonstrated those skills, then companies could be reasonably certain that they had identified a quality candidate.

2. **Companies had to ensure that they hired people and placed them in the right job where they would be utilizing their demonstrated skills, knowledge, and qualifications.**
   If a prospective employee's background indicated success in a particular type of job or job function, companies could be assured that they could place this new employee in a similar situation and he or she would do equally as well.

3. **Companies had to ensure that they hired people who would fit well into their corporate culture.**
   If a prospective employee had worked in a similar corporate environment in the past and performed well, then the new company could feel reasonably certain that the new employee would perform just as well within the organization.

4. **Companies had to ensure that they hired people who performed their jobs effectively and delivered results.**
   If a prospective employee had performed well in the past, a company could be confident that the new employee would also produce for their company.

Considering the above, it became readily apparent that previous behavior would be an excellent predictor of future behavior; thus, the development and proliferation of the practice of behavioral interviewing. This new practice changed the mindset of companies. Their focus transitioned from a strict review of past employment history to a more comprehensive review of the behaviors that prospective candidates demonstrated in those positions. Here's an example that will help clarify the concept:

Hiring Company: One of the world's largest telecommunications providers.

Situation: Company is expanding its incoming customer call center and needs experienced customer service trainers and relationship managers.

Hiring Requirements: An individual with a minimum of five years' experience in a similar, high-volume customer service environment and who has demonstrated outstanding staff training, problem solving, and customer management skills.

Demonstrated Behaviors: Following are demonstrated behaviors of Sally Moore, a prospective hire and the ideal candidate.

- **BEHAVIOR:** Trained more than 50 new employees over the past two years, providing both classroom lectures and on-the-job training. Redesigned classroom training programs to more accurately reflect actual work requirements and expanded orientation from two weeks to four. **RESULTS:** Resulted in a better than 90% retention of all new hires.

- **BEHAVIOR:** Personally handled all incoming calls from dissatisfied customers throughout the New England region. **RESULTS:** Successfully resolved service problems in cooperation with field personnel and retained more than 98% of all customers.

- **BEHAVIOR:** Hand-selected by Division Manager to participate in a special task force established to manage key customer relationships. **RESULTS:** Introduced six new products throughout customer base, resulting in new revenues of $250,000 within the first six months.

Although a relatively basic example, the above clearly illustrates how behavioral interviewing works and the type of information it provides to a prospective employer. Sally used her past work history to demonstrate that she did indeed have the *right* experience which the company was seeking by highlighting her actions (behaviors) and their results. In turn, this information allowed the hiring manager to predict her future behaviors within the organization.

KeyWords

As we have discussed at length in Chapters 1 and 2, KeyWords are the hot words associated with a specific industry, profession, or job function. They are nouns and noun phrases - that communicate a specific message about an individual's work experience. Here are a few examples to refresh your memory:

KeyWord/KeyWord Phrase	Message It Communicates
E-commerce	Technology-based sales, trade and commerce generally utilizing the Internet as the medium by which transactions are executed.
Staffing	Organizational needs assessment to determine requirements, followed by the recruitment, selection, and hiring of new employees.
Sourcing	Research, investigation, and selection of new vendors from which to purchase quality products at a competitive price.
Make/Buy Analysis	Evaluation of costs, personnel, and resources required to manufacture in-house as compared to the actual purchase of the same finished product or component from a secondary source.
Holistic Care	Integration of multiple patient care systems, processes, practices, and providers to create a health care protocol that encompasses the entire being.
In-Store Merchandising	Selection, display, and promotion of retail merchandise to the general buying public.
Sales Negotiations	Negotiation of product sales, pricing, and contract terms and conditions with prospective customers.

Cash Management   Control of incoming cash funds and their ap-
                                       propriate allocation to meet short- and long-
                                       term financial obligations.

If you would like to read more about KeyWord usage, please refer back to the earlier chapters in this book for a more comprehensive discussion of the history and use of KeyWords in today's job search market. In addition, feel free to look ahead at the chapters that highlight KeyWords specific to your industry and profession, and how to use these KeyWords for optimum interview performance.

KeyWord-Based Interviewing

As defined in the equation at the beginning of this chapter, KeyWord-based interviewing is the practice of using KeyWords to demonstrate behavioral competencies. It's that easy! Compare the following two responses to the question, "How many people did you supervise in your last position?"

Behavioral Response Without KeyWords:

I supervised a staff of 22 in the Accounting Department.

Behavioral Response With KeyWords:

As Delco's Accounting Manager, I hired, trained, and supervised a staff of 22 responsible for accounts payable, accounts receivable, monthly reconciliations, bank reconciliations, and cash management.

In the first response, the candidate has clearly demonstrated, through past behaviors, that he is experienced in supervising other employees. He has the right past behavior to indicate that he will be successful in supervising other employees at the new company.

The second response, however, is much more powerful! The candidate has used KeyWords to more effectively highlight his past behaviors which, as we've discussed, predict his future success using those same behaviors in other situations. In fact, there are a total of eight different KeyWords and KeyWord phrases in just that one sentence:

Accounting Manager	Accounts Payable
Monthly Reconciliations	Accounts Receivable
Bank Reconciliations	Hired
Cash Management	Trained

Here's another example using the question, "Are you PC proficient?"

Behavioral Response Without KeyWords:

> Yes, I have a great deal of PC experience from both of my last jobs and can learn to use new software very quickly.

Behavioral Response With KeyWords:

> Yes, I'm proficient with Microsoft Word, Access, Excel, PowerPoint, and Lotus, and have some hands-on experience working with PhotoShop, Quark Express, and WordPerfect. Most recently, I've been appointed to the PC Training Team at my current company where I'm responsible for one-on-one and group training on new PC software.

Again, the KeyWord response clearly outlines the candidate's experience and past behavior (PC proficiency) by highlighting the following KeyWords:

Microsoft Word	Access
Excel	PowerPoint
Lotus	PhotoShop
WordPerfect	Quark Express

Now, think for a moment how much information just one or two simple sentences can communicate to a prospective employer and you'll understand why KeyWord-based interviewing is the best strategy to use. KeyWord responses to interview questions give you the *power to perform* and immediately distinguish you from others competing for the same position. If you want the offer, then give the employer reasons to hire you by demonstrating that you have the right experience, qualifications, and track record of success.

Structuring Your Best KeyWord-Based Responses

Now that you understand what KeyWord-based interviewing is all about, let's look at the different types of KeyWord-based responses you can formulate to answer the diversity of questions you may be asked in an interview. How you answer each question will depend on what skills, qualifications, and experiences you have that are most related to that particular question and that best represent the value you bring to that company.

Basically, there are eight types of KeyWord-based interview responses:

1. Accomplishment Responses
2. Career-Change Responses
3. Historical/Chronological Responses
4. Overcoming-Objection Responses
5. Problem-Solving & Solution Responses
6. Project-Highlight Responses
7. Skills-Based Responses
8. Skirting-the-Issue Responses

To best demonstrate how to use each of these responses in actual interview situations, following are sample interview questions and answers illustrating each of the eight strategies.

Accomplishment Response
(KeyWord Phrase - Customer Satisfaction)

Question: Our company is currently ranked #1 in customer satisfaction in our industry. If we hire you, how can we be assured that your level of commitment to service and satisfaction is as strong as ours?

Your Response: That's easy. While employed as the Customer Service Manager for IBM's PC division, our customer satisfaction ranking improved from #5 to #2 in the industry. Then, under my leadership, Dell's customer satisfaction scores soared, from #8 to #1 in the home computer market. Most recently, I've taken a new technology company from virtual obscurity to #1 in the broadcast media market. I think these numbers speak for themselves and for my commitment to continually achieving #1 status.

Career-Change Response
(KeyWord Phrase - Performance Appraisals)

Question: Why, after so many years in sales management, would you want to consider a position managing the performance appraisal and promotion system within our HR department? We're having a difficult time understanding why you're interested in making such an abrupt career change.

Your Response: My answer to that question is really twofold. First of all, throughout my sales career, I have been directly responsible for performance appraisals and promotions for a sales team of up to 200 individuals. I have found this to be a particularly rewarding facet of my management responsibility and one that I take quite seriously. Having the opportunity to help younger professionals plan and develop their careers is a wonderful contribution to make to the success of any organization. Secondly, and on a personal note, I would like to return to San Diego and establish my new base here. After more than 20 years of living on the road and in hotels, I'm ready to live at home.

Historical/Chronological Response
(KeyWord Phrase - Information Systems Management)

Question: In looking for the right candidate to assume management responsibility for our IS department, we've decided that we're most interested in an individual who has risen through the ranks to their current management assignment. We believe this gives the individual a unique perspective as to what is involved in managing such a diverse operation. Can you please detail your career background?

Your Response: My career track is straightforward. I was recruited by Baltimore Gas & Electric immediately following graduation from the University of Baltimore and have remained with the company for the past 18 years. Starting as a Programmer, I advanced to Senior Programmer, Associate Project Manager, Senior Project Manager, IS Team Leader, and now my current position as Associate Manager of the entire IS operation. This is a 24/7 operation with more than 3,500 users on a daily basis accessing our systems and networks from locations throughout the state. Currently, I lead a staff of 32 programmers and project managers, and control an annual operating budget of $3.8 million. My career has been one of cumulative responsibilities, just as you're looking for. Beginning with a hands-on role and retaining that hands-on responsibility for years and years, I rose through the management ranks and am now poised for the #1 IS management position.

Overcoming-Objection Response
(KeyWord Phrase - Cash Management)

Question: I realize you've never been directly responsible for the corporate cash management function. Why do you think we should consider you for this position?

Your Response: There are basically three reasons. First, I do have substantial accounting experience including managing and reporting cash receivables, handling corporate banking functions, and assisting the CFO with a number of special projects designed to strengthen our cash position. Second, I am extremely organized and efficient, I have some supervisory experience along with lots of staff training experience, and I have excellent communication skills. Third, and perhaps most important, I'm a great employee and you'll be delighted to have me as part of your corporate finance team. When I left my last two positions for better opportunities, each time I was offered a promotion to stay with the company. I'm intelligent, I'm committed, and I will work intensely hard for you.

Problem-Solving & Solution Response
(KeyWord Phrase - Account Management)

Question: One of our greatest challenges is the management and retention of our account relationships as the volume of our competitors has increased. Can you elaborate on your experience in this area?

Your Response: My entire account management philosophy centers around the fact that in order to succeed, I must own the customer relationship. Specifically, I must position myself and the companies and products that I represent as sole-source providers to my accounts, meaning that no matter what their needs, I can meet them. By utilizing this approach, I have been extremely successful in the field. In my current position, I manage relationships with more than 100 wholesale accounts within the agricultural industry. Over the past year, I've retained 98% of my customers; the 2% who left went out of business. In my previous sales position with Heinhold Farms, I retained an average of 92% of my accounts for five consecutive years, despite increasing competition with lower pricing. My customers knew that I would deliver and that I would take care of them.

Project-Highlight Response
(KeyWord Phrase - Capital Projects)

Question: Now that we're planning a major expansion of our automotive plant, we're in need of a talented Project Manager with years of experience in capital projects. What have been some of the most notable projects that you've managed?

Your Response: Managing capital projects is what I do best and what I enjoy most. Here's a brief listing of some of my major projects: a $4 million renovation to Saturn's manufacturing plant, a $9.8 expansion of the Luxor complex in Las Vegas, a $2.3 million addition to IBM's corporate headquarters facility, and a $5 million new construction project on behalf of AT&T. As you can tell from the dollars involved, each of these was a major project involving hundreds of field personnel over a year or two time frame. What's most significant has been my financial success. Two of these projects were delivered within budget; one came in at $500,000 under budget, and the other at $1.8 million under budget. Considering the escalating costs of construction, these were notable achievements and the reason I've been personally selected to manage such large-scale capital projects.

Skills-Based Response
(KeyWord Phrase - Warehousing & Distribution)

Question: Please detail the most complex warehousing and distribution system you've ever managed and how well you managed it.

Your Response: Although I am responsible for warehousing, distribution, materials, and logistics in my current position, the assignment that most accurately reflects the depth of my experience was as a Warehouse Manager for Ryder Dedicated Logistics. In that position, I managed three warehouses in the Seattle area distributing products to 15 different retail clients throughout Washington, Oregon, California, Idaho, and Nevada. These were 24/7 operations receiving products from more than 100 suppliers. All products were documented upon receipt, stored in the appropriate areas of each warehouse, and then loaded and shipped to each customer destination. In total, we handled over two million tons of product annually. Most representative of my success in this position was the fact that we achieved and maintained a better than 95% on-time distribution to all 15 customers.

Skirting-the-Issue Response
(KeyWord Phrase - Credit Management)

Question: Since the departure of our Credit Manager six months ago, I have to be honest in telling you that our credit management department has been performing on a less than acceptable level. What can you do to remedy this?

Your Response: Without knowing the details about your department, it is difficult at this point to provide a step-by-step plan for corrective action. What I can share with you, however, is what I believe is critical to the success and efficient management of any credit organization. First and foremost, it is essential that we implement the policies and procedures necessary to limit our risks. All too often, banks are so concerned about increasing volume that marginal credit requests are approved. This is not a policy I support. Second, I believe that an organization must have a strictly enforced loan recovery department that is able to quickly identify potentially non-performing accounts and initiate action prior to them ever becoming workout situations. If we are able to manage the front end and control the back end, then the overall performance of the credit management department will be strong. Let me also add how critical it is that departmental personnel are well trained, that documentation is thorough, that regulations are strictly adhered to, and that we constantly monitor our status and performance.

KeyWords and the "What-If" Questions

Another strategy that employers often use when interviewing prospective candidates is the *what-if* question. This might include questions such as:

- What if a new competitor was coming into the region with a product line quite similar to ours? What specific actions would you initiate to protect your customer base and revenue stream?

- What if the production output were to fall by 10% in just one week? What would you do?

- What if one of your department supervisors overspent her budget and had no funds for the remaining three months of the fiscal year? What would you do?

These types of questions provide a wealth of information to a prospective employer about your behaviors, your competencies, your knowledge about a specific job function, your thought process, the way your prioritize your workload, the manner in which you communicate with your employees and co-workers, and so much more. There are occasions when you'll be able to relate your past experiences and behaviors in responding to these questions if you have experience dealing with that particular situation. There will, however, be just as many occasions where your focus will be strictly on your future behaviors (what you would do in that situation) if you've never been presented with that particular challenge.

To better explain, let's answer each of the above questions, using KeyWords and/or past behaviors to demonstrate future behaviors.

- *What if a new competitor was coming into the region with a product line quite similar to ours? What specific actions would you initiate to protect your customer base and revenue stream?*

In my current position as Territory Sales Manager with the Phoenix Group, I encountered that exact same situation last year. Phoenix was well-entrenched within the Dallas market and had enjoyed #1 ranking for the past two years. Then, a major competitor appeared on the scene and launched a multi-million dollar consumer marketing campaign. In order to ensure that our customer base was protected, I personally contacted all 215 of our key accounts to further solidify my relationship with them and halt any ideas they may have had about jumping ship. Then, to ensure that we continued to grow, I spearheaded a number of new business development initiatives and a region-wide print and broadcast advertising campaign. As a result, not only did we retain our entire customer base, my team and I closed an additional $2 million in revenues that year and continue to be ranked #1 in the region.

If we dissect the above response, we're presented with:

Behaviors & Actions: I personally contacted all 215 of our key accounts to further solidify my relationship with them and halt any ideas they may have had about jumping ship....I spearheaded a number of new business development initiatives and a region-wide print and broadcast advertising campaign.

Results: Not only did we retain our entire customer base, my team and I closed an additional $2 million in revenues that year and continue to be ranked as #1 in the region.

KeyWords & KeyWord Phrases: Territory Sales Manager, Marketing Campaign, Customer Base, Key Accounts, New Business Development, Print and Broadcast Advertising Campaign, Revenues

- *What if the production output were to fall by 10% in just one week? What would you do?*

Fortunately, I've never been presented with such a serious problem that occurred so rapidly. However, if that were to happen, I would immediately begin a comprehensive analysis of all key functions within my production area, from pre-production planning and scheduling to materials acquisition to full production floor operations. This would allow me to quickly and accurately identify the function or functions slowing production. I would assemble personnel representing each department to form an emergency task force that focused on each key function in anticipation that a cross-functional team approach would be the most efficient and most effective for rapid problem identification and action planning. Realizing that a problem of such magnitude could potentially be devastating to the company, the analysis and resulting corrective actions would be undertaken immediately to restore production yields and ensure the financial viability of the company.

Behaviors & Actions: I would immediately begin a comprehensive analysis of all key functions within my production area, from pre-production planning and scheduling to materials acquisition and movement to full production floor operations, in an effort to quickly and accurately identify the function or functions slowing production.I would assemble personnel representing each department to form an emergency task force that focused on each key function in anticipation that a cross-functional team approach would be the most efficient and most effective for rapid problem identification and action planning.

Results: The analysis and resulting corrective actions would be undertaken almost immediately in order to restore production yields and ensure the financial viability of the company.

KeyWords & KeyWord Phrases: Pre-Production Planning and Scheduling, Materials Acquisition and Movement, Production Floor Operations, Task Force, Cross-Functional Team Approach, Problem Identification, Action Planning, Corrective Actions, Production Yields, Financial Viability

- *What if one of your department supervisors overspent her budget and had no funds for the remaining three months of the fiscal year? What would you do?*

During my tenure as Macy's Buyer Manager for 125 stores in the Northeastern U.S., I was faced with a similar problem when one of my buyers overspent her annual budget in just six months. As such, we were left with no funds at all for any children's clothing lines at any of our stores. It was a serious situation that really required two distinct actions. First and foremost, I had to get the clothing into the stores in order to meet our projected customer demand. I investigated the possibility of additional funding, but quickly discovered that would not be an option. I then assembled three of my top buyers and together we readjusted budgets between all the various departments to provide the additional funding that was needed.

Once merchandise was again arriving from our suppliers, I pulled the children's clothing buyer from the field and re-enrolled her in the company's three-month buyer training program. In other instances, I might have reassigned the employee to a less responsible position or even let her go; however, this employee had demonstrated excellent success in contract negotiations, supplier communications, and merchandise selection. She was worth keeping. The net results of my actions were twofold: We retained a qualified employee who subsequently performed quite well when she returned to her position; perhaps more important, we were able to meet all of our sales goals for the entire children's clothing line that year.

Behaviors & Actions: I investigated the possibility of additional funding, but quickly discovered that would not be an option. I then assembled three of my top buyers and together we readjusted budgets between all the various departments to provide the additional funding that was needed….I pulled the children's clothing buyer from the field and re-enrolled her in the company's three-month buyer training program.

Results: We retained a qualified employee who subsequently performed quite well when she returned to her position.…We were able to meet all of our sales goals for the entire children's clothing line that year.

KeyWords & KeyWord Phrases: Buyer Manager, Budget, Customer Demand, Funding, Merchandising, Buyer Training, Contract Negotiations, Supplier Communications, Sales Goals

As you can readily see from the above examples, KeyWord-based interview responses that clearly communicate the behaviors you've demonstrated in the past or anticipate in the future, are excellent predictors of your success on the job. Your challenge, then, is to redefine how you think about the interview process, how you can use past behaviors to indicate your future performance, and how you can integrate KeyWords to your advantage. If you are able to master the art of

KeyWord-based interviewing, you will have mastered one of the most critical components in the entire job search process.

Top 10 Tips for the Perfect Interview

No book on interviewing would be complete without a brief discussion of the top 10 tips for interview success. If you can effectively integrate the practice of KeyWord-based interviewing with the following recommendations, you will consistently win in each and every interview situation.

1. **Build Rapport.** The single most important thing that you can accomplish during an interview is to build instant rapport with your interviewer. Sometimes this can be readily accomplished in just a moment or two. Suppose you enter the HR manager's office and the first thing you notice on the wall is a picture of the manager on the baseball field. Coincidentally, you played pro ball years ago, right out of college. Instantly, the two of you have a mutual interest and the rapport begins to build.

Sometimes, however, it's not quite that readily apparent. Instead of relying on external cues to begin to bond with your interviewer, you'll have to let the conversation work for you and let the rapport develop through your manner of communication and your responses to particular interview questions.

2. **Quickly identify the company's specific challenges and issues.** In any interview situation, you are there to answer questions, provide information, explore the job opportunity, highlight your skills and successes, and position yourself as the #1 candidate. However, JUST AS IMPORTANT, you are there to listen to your interviewer, understand his concerns, and then, respond directly to those issues. This can be a difficult challenge since so much of your energy is focused on answering the interviewer's questions as opposed to hearing what the interviewer is saying.

   Your interviewer will most likely communicate information about the position, the company, the major issues impacting the company, the need to fill the position, and the qualifications for the ideal candidate. Listen carefully to all of this information and then use it wisely in positioning your responses to each interview question. Your objective is to highlight the specific behaviors, qualifications, achievements, KeyWords, and more that clearly demonstrate your capabilities as they relate to each specific item that is addressed. If you can do this, you will win!

3. **Listen carefully.** Everyone wants to be listened to and heard, and your interviewer is no different.If your interviewer knows that you are hearing what she's saying, you have immediately communicated a message of interest and commitment. People want to hire other people who understand them, support them, and are sensitive to their needs. Position yourself above the crowd by not only communicating your competencies, but responding to the company's specific needs.

4. **Take notes.** Taking notes during an interview is a well-accepted practice and one that I recommend. By taking notes, you've accomplished two very important things. First, you're communicating to your interviewer that you are interested in the position, in the company, and in what he is saying. Second, you're creating a resource of important comments, issues, challenges, and qualifications that you can then use when writing your thank-you-after-the-interview letter.

5. **Successfully answer the "tell-me-about-yourself" question.** There are two strategies that you can use to answer the infamous "tell me about yourself" question. The first approach - the passive approach - is to provide your interviewer with a brief summation of your career history. Your answer may begin with, "When I graduated from Southern Illinois University in 1991, I accepted an entry-level financial analysis position with Boise Cascade where I stayed for three years and earned two promotions. Following that, I accepted an opportunity with Johnson & Johnson in their corporate accounting department where I was responsible for divisional budgeting, cash flow management, and long-range financial forecasting. Then, in 1998, I was recruited to…" When proceeding in this fashion, you talk your interviewer through your entire career track. This is not the strategy that I recommend.

More modern thought has changed the strategy for answering that question. Instead of reciting your career history which is already clearly displayed on your resume, I recommend you use a more active approach by summarizing who you are today and the value you bring to the hiring company. Suppose, for example, that you're a senior executive within the technology industry. When answering that question, you might respond with:

"I am a well-qualified senior executive who has met the unique challenges of start-up, turnaround, and high-growth companies. Never working in what one would consider a status quo organization, I have continually been challenged to deliver results that required strong creative, strategic, and tactical leadership talents.Most significant, in each and every one of these situations, I increased revenues and market share, reduced costs, and improved bottom-line profitability.

"A few specific examples that best exemplify my performance include my current leadership of an early-stage technology venture for which I have generated $45 million in new revenues within one year. In my previous position as the General Manager of the Partners-in-Technology Division of X-Tech, my team and I not only improved profitability 25% but also positioned the company as #1 in the national market. Earlier career achievements were equally notable in sales, marketing, turnarounds, and new venture development.

"In summary, I consider myself a consummate management professional, confident in my ability to tackle virtually any challenge by assembling the right personnel, identifying the appropriate markets, and building product recognition despite competition. Of paramount importance to my success has been my ability to build relationships throughout all levels of an organization, defining common goals, implementing incentives, and challenging my workforce to deliver its best."

With the above, more active response to the question, you get a much clearer sense of the candidate's skills, qualifications, achievements, and proposed value to the new company. Work to develop your active response to this often-asked question and you'll immediately position yourself above the competition.

6. **Know how to use your accomplishments to sell your success.** Interviewing is basically a selling game. You have a product to sell - yourself - and your goal is to market that product as effectively as possible. Don't just tell your interviewer that "Yes, I managed annual budgeting for the division." Rather, sell the fact that "For the past three years, I have independently managed the entire budgeting function for a $22 million operating division during which time I initiated a series of cost-reduction programs that have saved the company more than $3 million in annual operating expenses." In the first response, you told the facts. In the second response, you sold the success.

7. **Realize that not all accomplishments are quantifiable.** Not every accomplishment or success is quantifiable and that's okay! No interviewer expects it to be any different. Of course, if you're in sales, chances are you can talk revenue dollars, budgets, and sales goals. On the other hand, if you're an attorney, your achievements will generally not focus on quantifiable numbers, but rather on the depth and breadth of your legal expertise, big cases you've won, legal precedents you've helped establish, and the like. Let yourself off the hook and realize that an achievement does not have to have a number associated with it to be a success!

8. **Use the big-to-little strategy.** Putting structure into your interview responses will make the process easier, more manageable, and more effective. Begin your answers with a big response and then follow up with specific little examples that demonstrate your proficiency. Consider the following example from a candidate who was asked about his experience managing information technology resources. His response began with the big comment, "Throughout the past eight years, I have held full planning, staffing, operating and management responsibility for a 48-person IT organization." Now, onto the little with "Specific highlights that may be of interest to you include a $3.8 million investment in e-commerce and teleconferencing technology, establishment of the company's first-ever global telecommunications network, and the recruitment and retention of two Ph.D.-educated systems engineers to guide our long-range technology planning programs."

    This type of structured response allows your interviewer to immediately capture the overall scope of your experience as well as understand how you have used your knowledge within a specific work situation. Again, you've made the interviewer's job so much easier by clearly communicating the behaviors and actions that you have demonstrated.

9. **Take the initiative.** If there is information that you believe is important to communicate to your interviewer, be sure to take the initiative and introduce the topic into the conversation when appropriate. If you are nearing the end of your interview and the topic has not been addressed, tell your interviewer that there are several other points you would like to address and ask if this would be a good time. If you don't take the initiative, chances are the topic may never come out and you will have failed to communicate important information.

10. **Be positive, confident, and self-assured.** Companies want to hire winners, and winners communicate an immediate message of confidence in their qualifications, skills, abilities, and performance. Be sure that you convey this message through both your verbal and nonverbal communications. A strong handshake, direct eye contact, and a smile readily communicate poise, confidence, and self-assurance.

Now that we've completed our discussion of what KeyWord-based interviewing is all about, we're ready to move on to the specific KeyWord interviews for 16 different industries, professions, and job functions highlighted in this book. Those 16 are:

- Accounting & Finance
- Banking & Investment

- Customer Service
- Education
- Engineering
- Health Care
- Hospitality
- Human Resources
- Human Services
- International Business
- Legal
- Manufacturing
- Retail
- Sales & Marketing
- Senior Management & Executives
- Technology

Each chapter is laid out in the same format and structure with the following information included for all 16 professions:

Part I - *Listing of Top 10 KeyWords*

Part II - *KeyWord Interview Questions & Answers (Q&A)*

Part III - *KeyWord Accomplishment Phrases for Your Interviews, Resumes, & Cover Letters*

Study and use these KeyWords and KeyWord Phrases to your advantage to powerfully and successfully manage your KeyWord-based interviews. You have the tools and resources in your hand; now you have to make it happen!

Chapter 4

KeyWords for the Accounting & Finance Professional

Top 10 KeyWords and KeyWord Phrases

Asset & Liability Management
Auditing
Budgeting
Cash Management
Cost Accounting
Financial Analysis
Financial Reporting
General Accounting
Mergers & Acquisitions
Treasury

KeyWord Interview Q&A

Asset & Liability Management

Question: One of the critical issues facing our company is the accurate recording, management, and control of all of our corporate assets and liabilities. Can you address your experience in this area?

Your Response: When I joined ARMCO in 2002, the company had experienced tremendous growth over the past several years as a result of more than 20 acquisitions. Needless to say, integrating all the financial systems of these companies was a huge undertaking to which more than 50 finance and accounting personnel were assigned. My direct responsibility was the timely and seamless integration and consolidation of all asset and liability management systems into one global system for the entire corporation. Using a collaborative approach, I established a financial analysis team to dissect the specific operations of each individual system, a new systems team responsible for establishing standards and conformity, and an IT project team to support our efforts. Most notable is the fact that I took this project from concept to completion in just six months.

Auditing

Question: Does your experience include both internal and external auditing?

Your Response: Yes. While working for Andersen, I managed annual external audit engagements for about 25 clients in the textile industry. Now, in my position with Bose, I coordinate internal audit engagements for more than 50 company locations in the U.S., Canada, Latin America, and the Far East. Most significant is that all of my internal audits have passed external examinations with no audit findings. Considering the diversity of the workforce, corporate cultures, languages, and other factors, I consider this to be one of my most significant career achievements.

Budgeting

Question: One of the reasons that we're most interested in you is because of your apparent success in controlling budget overruns. Can you elaborate on your experience?

Your Response: Somehow, unintentionally, that has become the hallmark of my career at Emerson Electric! Here's a brief history of how that happened. When I joined the company in 1994, one of my first assignments was as a Project Accountant for a $12 million construction project that was way over budget.By rearranging project scheduling and monitoring field work on a daily basis, I restored the project to its original budget and actually closed it at $200,000 less! My manager was thrilled! He then asked me to look at an upcoming project proposal that was just about ready to be signed. Again, by rescheduling and a few basic, but critical, design change recommendations, we cut the project budget $1.8 million. At that point, the corporate purchasing department had heard of my success and offered me a budget management position. To date, I have slashed an average of 12% from each year's composite purchasing budget through better vendor selection, more aggressive negotiations, and a firm stand on the quality and performance we require of each supplier.

Cash Management

Question: I realize you've never been directly responsible for the corporate cash management function. Why do you think we should consider you for this position?

Your Response: There are basically three reasons. First, I do have substantial accounting experience including managing and reporting cash receivables, handling corporate banking functions, and assisting the CFO with a number of special projects designed to strengthen our cash position. Second, I am extremely organized and efficient, I have some supervisory experience along with lots of staff training experience, and I have excellent communication skills. Third, and perhaps most important, I'm a great employee and you'll be delighted to have me as part of your corporate finance team. When I left my last two positions for better opportunities, each time I was offered a promotion to stay with the company. I'm intelligent, I'm committed, and I will work intensely hard for you.

Cost Accounting

Question: To be perfectly honest, our cost accounting system is in dire need of a complete redesign. The technology is antiquated, it does not provide our production management team with the kind of information they so critically need, and it certainly doesn't generate the detailed financial data we need for long-range planning. How can you help?

Your Response: I can help in several different ways. However, let me begin by sharing the fact that I have been directly responsible for the entire cost accounting function for Shaklee's flagship production facility. Over the past five years, I have orchestrated two major technology upgrades along with several smaller projects to create what is considered one of the industry's leading cost accounting systems. Secondly, much like your requirements, I have completely redesigned the data capture, analysis, and reporting function to ensure that both production and management teams have immediate access to critical financial and planning data. And it's worked! Within the past three years, our productivity has increased 16% while our operating costs have been reduced an average of 11% annually. I guarantee I can do the same for you.

Financial Analysis

Question: Let's be honest. Sitting in an office, compiling financial data and completing detailed financial analyses is not a particularly exciting job. What makes you think you'll be satisfied with such a position?

Your Response: First of all, I love numbers, data, facts, and figures. Believe it or not, I do find it exciting and have always known that financial planning and analysis is what I would do for a living. At Duke, I majored in finance, minored in economics, and graduated with a 3.95 GPA on a 4.0 scale. During my internship with Siemens, I spent six months in their financial analysis division, reviewing and reporting on operating costs and capital expenditures, and thoroughly enjoyed each moment of it. In fact, I was offered a full-time, professional position when I graduated, but due to family obligations, I wanted to return to Indianapolis. I guarantee you that I'll never be bored, but will expect rapid advancement based on my performance.

Financial Reporting

Question: Currently, we have six autonomous financial reporting systems for each of our six operating divisions. Although the system has worked well for us in the past, it's now time to integrate. The greatest problem we have encountered is building consensus on the new financial reporting systems and models, and, as such, the process has stalled. How can you help?

Your Response: Change is always difficult in any environment. One of the most valuable lessons I've learned in my career is that to facilitate major change requires two key components – the active participation of the individuals and departments the change will impact, and a series of small steps that take the project from step one all the way through completion. I never recommend that massive changes are initiated in one huge undertaking. Rather, I prefer to meet with all the parties, create an action plan with full buy-in, and then manage that project in such a manner that each person feels as though his or her needs are being met and they're not overwhelmed with totally new work requirements.

General Accounting

Question: Please expand on your experience in managing the general accounting office for your current employer.

Your Response: In my current position, the scope of my responsibility is extensive and includes accounts payable, accounts receivable, monthly reconciliations, bank reconciliations, cash management, and budget reporting. In addition, I coordinate all departmental hiring, training, personnel evaluations, and promotions, along with all new technology installations and software upgrades. Then, in my spare time, I also assist the CFO with some of his special projects. This included a recent audit examination of our inventory function that identified a little over $400,000 in inventory losses and reduced our corporate tax liability accordingly.

Mergers & Acquisitions

Question: One of the most critical components of this position is leading our merger and acquisition projects. I noticed on your resume that you were responsible for M&A activity at both of your last positions, but you didn't elaborate. Can you do so now?

Your Response: In total, over the past five years, I have personally led 12 major M&A projects in the information technology, videoconferencing, and telecommunications industries with a total investment of well over $500 million. My role in each project has been comprehensive, from the initial identification and evaluation of prospective M&A targets, through complex due diligence reviews of products, technologies, and financials, through to contract development, pricing, negotiations, and contract closing. These have been wonderful experiences that have allowed me to travel the world, operate in a diversity of business cultures, and establish relationships with foreign officials never before approached by our company. Characterized by others as a consummate dealmaker, I thoroughly enjoy the challenge, appreciate the hard work, and delight in closing the deal.

Treasury

Question: Our treasury functions have come under close scrutiny from a number of regulatory agencies. As such, we're most concerned about recruiting a new Treasurer with not only the financial expertise, but also the requisite experience in working with federal and state government officials. What has been your experience in managing these relationships?

Your Response: Throughout my corporate finance and treasury career, I have interfaced with officials from the federal and state governments, as well as from several foreign countries in Europe. As we discussed in our telephone interview, I have the depth and quality of treasury experience you're seeking in a qualified candidate. I think we've established that. Therefore, what distinguishes me most from others with a similar background, is my specific ability to build cooperative working relationships with regulators, respond appropriately to their requirements and directives, immediately resolve any problems or concerns, and ensure that we maintain 100% compliance. In fact, I've found that these individuals really can be your ally if the relationship is cooperative, not confrontational. This is the greatest value I bring to your organization.

KeyWord Accomplishment Phrases for Interviews, Resumes, and Cover Letters

Asset & Liability Management

- Managed a $450,000 asset portfolio and $1.2 million in short- and long-term liabilities as KMart reorganized its operations, realigned staffing patterns, and restructured inventory planning and acquisition. Maintained asset value while reducing corporate debt by more than $250,000.

Auditing

- Planned, staffed, budgeted, and directed annual audit engagements for 25 key clients of Gemini Consulting. Delivered all engagements on time and within budget despite often difficult staffing situations and time-sensitive commitments critical to retaining client relationships.

Budgeting

- Managed a $45 million annual operating budget for Maulden Mills and a $3.5 million annual capital expense budget allocated for facilities improvement/expansion projects and technology acquisitions. Achieved all budget objectives for eight consecutive years while reducing annual capital expenses by more than 20%.

Cash Management

- Realigned corporate cash management systems to improve liquidity and meet all short-term obligations. Created cash management model subsequently incorporated into all four divisions of the company worldwide.

Cost Accounting

- Designed and implemented new cost accounting system integrating all operating, payroll, and overhead costs with plant-wide expenses. Effort resulted in a 12% increase in net profitability by eliminating unnecessary expenses.

Financial Analysis

- Created best-in-class financial analysis systems which were critical in halting Weyerhauser's anticipated acquisition of its largest competitor. Identified critical data which negated the proposed profitability of the acquisition.

Financial Reporting

- Developed new financial reporting methodology which integrated two independent accounting systems with a newly implemented corporate-wide financial management system, reduced staffing requirements 22%, and enhanced the quality and timeliness of all financial data reported to senior management team.

General Accounting

- Led all general accounting functions including payables, receivables, general ledger, quarterly and annual reporting, and cash control for a $200,000 professional services company. Automated previously manual functions to improve data access and reliability.

Mergers & Acquisitions

- Spearheaded the entire corporate development function including mergers, acquisitions, joint ventures, strategic alliances, and technology transfers during Tyco's rapid ascension into the top five telecommunications companies in the world. Over the past four years, personally structured, negotiated, and closed 12 M&A transactions along with scores of smaller JV, alliance, and technology transfer projects.

Treasury

- Recruited to revitalize SYSCO's corporate treasury function, renegotiate core banking relationships, and redesign cash management, foreign exchange, and currency hedging programs. Key contributor to 32% increase in the company's stock valuation.

Your Personal KeyWord Toolkit

Use the space on the next page to add in KeyWords and KeyWord Phrases from your own career in Accounting & Finance. Once you've done that, you'll want to do three more things essential to the success of your job search campaign.

1. Write KeyWord accomplishment phrases for each new KeyWord and KeyWord Phrase on your list. Then, use those words in your resume, cover letters, and interviews.

2. Write KeyWord interview responses to use when each of those KeyWord topics comes up. That way, you'll be instantly prepared with answers that effectively highlight your accomplishments, key projects, record of promotion, honors and awards, and other distinguishing aspects of your career.

3. Practice #1 and #2 above over and over! Although it certainly isn't necessary that you memorize each and every accomplishment and interview response, it is essential that the moment the topic comes up during an interview, you're immediately prepared to answer.

Your KeyWords & KeyWord Phrases:

_____

_____

_____

_____

_____

_____

_____

_____

_____

_____

Chapter 5

KeyWords for the Banking & Investment Professional

Top 10 KeyWords & KeyWord Phrases

Commercial Banking
Commercial Credit
Credit Management
Deposits
Foreign Exchange
Investment Management
Lending & Loan Administration
Portfolio Management
Private Banking
Retail Banking

KeyWord Interview Q&A

Commercial Banking

Question: We want a top producer in this position…an individual with substantial experience in commercial banking and the ability to perform within an intensely competitive market. Are you that candidate?

Your Response: Yes, without a doubt, I am your candidate. When I began my commercial banking career in 1989, I started small, managing financial analysis functions for one of the nation's largest banks. In just six years, I was promoted five times and then offered an exceptional management opportunity with Mellon Bank. Today, as one of the top executives managing Mellon's commercial banking operations, I have enjoyed tremendous success. Our customer base has grown by better than 35% over the past four years, deposits and loan volume are at an all-time high, and our shareholders are delighted with our bottom-line financial performance. Yes, I can manage commercial banking operations, improve quality of service, increase profits, and ensure your long-term market lead.

Commercial Credit

Question: If I were to give you full responsibility for all commercial credit functions at our institution, how could I be assured that you would be able to manage such a large and diverse department?

Your Response: I believe that my track record of performance highlights my capabilities. Not only have I managed commercial credit functions for two of the region's largest banking institutions, I have delivered measurable results for both. During my tenure with SunTrust, the dollar volume of our commercial credit transactions increased 35% over three years while credit write-offs decreased 12%. Currently, as the Director of Commercial Credit for The Bank of the James, I built the function from start-up to its current volume of more than $8.9 million in outstanding credit transactions with less than 5% bad debt performance. I am both manager and financier, able to juggle my two roles as necessary to ensure the integrity of our institution and the satisfaction of our corporate clients.

Credit Management

Question: Since the departure of our Credit Manager six months ago, I have to be honest in telling you that our credit management department has been performing on a less than acceptable level. What can you do to remedy this?

Your Response: Without knowing the details about your department, it is difficult at this point to provide a step-by-step plan for corrective action. What I can share with you, however, is what I believe to be critical to the success and efficient management of any credit organization. First and foremost, it is essential that we implement the policies and procedures necessary to limit our risks. All too often, banks are so concerned about increasing volume that marginal credit requests are approved. This is not a policy

I support. Second, I believe that an organization must have a strictly enforced loan workout department that is able to quickly identify potentially non-performing accounts and initiate action prior to them ever becoming workout situations. If we are able to manage the front end and control the back end, then the overall performance of the credit management department will be strong. Let me also add how critical it is that departmental personnel are well trained, that documentation is thorough, that regulations are strictly adhered to, and that we constantly monitor our status and performance.

Deposits

Question: As a Branch Manager, I assume you've been responsible for all facets of the bank's operations. What I'm most interested in is your experience in building deposit volume. Can you please address how you've been able to accomplish that?

Your Response: Building our deposits has resulted from the unique combination of our marketing and customer care programs. When we talk about deposit growth, we're really focused on two entirely different customer markets - our existing customer base as well as others who have never had the pleasure of working with First Union before. As such, I have always approached growth in deposits, loans, customer accounts and more, from two entirely different perspectives. On the one hand, I have created a bank culture that embraces its customers and is committed to the utmost in service. Conversely, it is also my responsibility to bring new customers and new deposits to our branch through a combination of marketing, advertising, and community outreach efforts. We have excelled in this area, bringing in more than $1.8 million in new customer deposits last year alone.

Foreign Exchange

Question: As Amazon.com has expanded its operations worldwide and entered into several large-scale joint ventures, it has become obvious to our financial management team that we need to bring in an expert in foreign exchange. Please elaborate on your experience in this area.

Your Response: Managing foreign exchange, currency hedging, and international business transactions is what I do best. As a member of the World Bank's economic development team, I have personally handled billions of dollars in FX transactions in more than 50 countries worldwide. It's been a great experience and paved the way for my interest in your position. Not only do I bring you a wealth of experience in FX, I also have substantial experience in joint ventures, mergers and acquisitions, and understand the unique financing requirements of each. Please also note that of particular value to you are the personal relationships I have developed with leading banks and banking officials worldwide. These relationships have been essential in allowing the World Bank to manage such complex international FX and trade transactions.

Investment Management

Question: Now that we're expanding our banking operations to include a full-service brokerage, we're looking to staff the function with individuals with extensive investment management experience. Can you address your experience in that area?

Your Response: A 12-year employee of Smith Barney, I have built an entire career in investment management. In particular, I am experienced in investment sales, portfolio development and management, trading, regulatory reporting, and customer relationship management. Although my different positions have focused on different aspects of the investment management function, all 12 of my years have been within that department. What's more, I have been actively involved in the start-up of a new investment department, specializing in foreign investments throughout Europe and Asia. For that project, I handled all staffing functions, designed training programs to educate personnel in the various foreign investment vehicles, coordinated development of documentation and reporting standards, and continue to provide overall strategic leadership as the department grows and expands worldwide. The combination of my expertise in the investment management discipline, along with my success in launching new departments, positions me as a prime candidate for your new assignment.

Lending & Loan Administration

Question: It appears as though your background has all been in consumer lending. However, this position is in our corporate lending and loan administration department. Why do you believe you're qualified for this position?

Your Response: After six years in consumer lending and loan administration, I'm ready to take the next step. I have clearly demonstrated my competencies in sales and new business development, customer relationship management, loan review and approval, loan documentation, and loan administration, the same skills one needs in corporate lending. Yes, the audience may be different and the documentation somewhat more complex. However, the underlying skill sets are the same and those are what I bring to this position, along with ambition, dedication, and the ability to quickly and accurately learn new information. I guarantee you that I'll be an asset to your corporate lending department.

Portfolio Management

Question: What is the largest portfolio you've ever managed and for whom?

Your Response: As a Fund Manager with Fidelity, I currently manage a portfolio of $350 million in mutual funds, stocks, and annuities on behalf of individual investors. Over the past two years, despite the overall poor performance within our economic markets, I have delivered annual investment returns of up to 23%. Previously, during my tenure with Global Investors Fund, I managed an institutional portfolio of more than $500 million in corporate and government bonds, and again achieved positive returns for three consecutive years. Most important is my strength in fund management, knowing what to buy, what to sell, and how to improve my results.

Private Banking

Question: We're just launching our first-ever private banking department and looking for a candidate who can assume full responsibility for this project. Are you qualified for such an assignment?

Your Response: Not only am I qualified, but I'm your perfect candidate! When I joined Wachovia two years ago, I was tasked with the development, implementation, and management of their first private banking operation. It was a particularly complex assignment given the fact that Wachovia was in the midst of a merger with First Union which, in and of itself, created a great deal of transition within the organization. Knowing that my private banking operation would impact personnel and resources at both banks, I initiated the project with personnel from both institutions, knowing that we would be one bank within a year. I then wrote the strategic plan for the new business unit, established all operating policies and procedures, hand-selected personnel from throughout the organization to staff our private banking function, and launched a massive marketing and business development campaign. Two years later, we have a well-established private banking operation, service more than 2,000 corporate clients, and handle billions of dollars in deposit, loan, and investment transactions.

Retail Banking

Question: Retail banking operations have become increasingly competitive as a result of the massive merger and acquisition activity in our industry. What do you think you can do to improve our retail banking operations?

Your Response: As many of us in the industry are aware, your bank is having a difficult time competing against the major players and retaining market share. It's a similar situation for many smaller banks and one that can be controlled by returning to the days of personalized retail banking. Of course, there is a place for PC banking, ATMs, and other non-human bank interactions. However, there is nothing that will ever replace the person-to-person contact of retail branch banking. I talk to my customers and I know how much they value that interaction and personal touch. As such, I believe that it's critical that we re-introduce many of the retail banking programs that have been lost as technology has taken over so much of our industry. If we are able to connect with our customers, let them know how much we value their business, and be available to answer questions and personally handle transactions, I guarantee new customers will be flocking to your bank. It worked for Crestar and I can make it work for you.

KeyWord Accomplishment Phrases for Interviews, Resumes, and Cover Letters

Branch Management

- Realigned SunTrust's entire branch management infrastructure, eliminated non-productive staff, consolidated non-essential operations, instituted pay-for-performance incentives, and reduced annual operating costs by better than 13%.

Commercial Banking

- Spearheaded the start-up of a de novo commercial banking institution that grew from start-up to over $450 million in deposits and $1.2 billion in assets within the first five years.

Commercial Credit

- Led loan processing staff of 12 responsible for the evaluation and approval of over $250 million in commercial credit transactions within a 6-month period, exceeding commercial lending goals by more than $50 million.

Credit Management

- Planned, staffed, budgeted, and led the start-up of a credit management organization in Singapore as part of First Mountain Bank's global expansion and diversification effort. Generated $2.2 million in fee income within the first 18 months of operation.

Deposits

- Launched a massive new business development initiative throughout the Los Angeles metro area, captured $50 million in new deposits within first two months, and won the bank's "Sales & Customer Service Recognition Award" for outstanding field performance.

Foreign Exchange

- Directed over $500 million in foreign exchange, currency hedging, and international lending transactions with no disruption in customer service despite the internal changes experienced during First Union's merger with Wachovia.

Investment Portfolio

- Managed a $2.2 billion investment portfolio comprised of blue-chip stocks, blue-chip mutual funds, and other long-term, high-yield products. Averaged 12% to 15% annual returns despite overall performance market performance in 2002 and 2003.

Loan Administration

- Promoted within two years of hire to administer Bank of America's retail loan programs for all 1,500+ branch offices throughout the U.S. Total portfolio valued in excess of $9.8 million.

Private Banking

- Led the start-up of the bank's first-ever private banking operations and built from start-up to over 250 corporate customers with total deposits of $300 million and total outstanding loans of more than $2.5 billion.

Retail Banking

- Positioned First Union as the largest retail banking operation in the Southwestern U.S. through a series of strategic sales, marketing, and business development efforts that captured 1,500+ new customers over 18 months.

Your Personal KeyWord Toolkit

Use the space below to add in KeyWords and KeyWord Phrases from your own career in Banking & Investment. Once you've done that, you'll want to do three more things essential to the success of your job search campaign.

1. Write KeyWord accomplishment phrases for each new KeyWord and KeyWord Phrase on your list. Then, use those words in your resume, cover letters, and interviews.

2. Write KeyWord interview responses to use when each of those KeyWord topics comes up. That way, you'll be instantly prepared with answers that effectively highlight your accomplishments, key projects, record of promotion, honors and awards, and other distinguishing aspects of your career.

3. Practice #1 and #2 above over and over! Although it certainly isn't necessary that you memorize each and every accomplishment and interview response, it is essential that the moment the topic comes up during an interview, you're immediately prepared to answer.

Your KeyWords & KeyWord Phrases:

_____

_____

_____

_____

Chapter 6

KeyWords for the
Customer Service Professional

Top 10 KeyWords & KeyWord Phrases

Customer Communications
Customer Loyalty
Customer Relationship Management
Customer Retention
Customer Satisfaction
Inbound Customer Service Operations
Order Processing & Fulfillment
Outbound Customer Service Operations
Sales Administration
Service Quality

KeyWord Interview Q&A

Customer Communications

Question: One of our primary missions is to create a comprehensive, multimedia customer communications program. Can you detail any
specific experience you've had in this area?

Your Response: Over the past year, one of the challenges of my department has
been to create a complete portfolio of customer communications.
Based on my past experience working on such projects, my
manager selected me to coordinate a team effort to develop print
brochures, print and online advertisements, direct mail pieces,
product videos, and a totally new website. I selected a graphic

designer, webmaster, copywriter, marketing analyst, and sales associate to staff the project team, and have led their efforts for the past nine months.To date, we have completed 16 print brochures and advertisements, scores of online ad pieces, and two new product videos. In addition, we have two new videos in production, and our new, 42-page website is scheduled for launch in just three weeks.

Customer Loyalty

Question: Our competition has been increasing at an unprecedented rate and it is critical that we focus on strengthening customer loyalty to both our company and our brand. Can you share any insights you may have in relation to how we might accomplish this?

Your Response: I believe that one of the most basic tenets of customer loyalty is learning to embrace each customer. Let me explain. Each and every time a customer has any contact with the company, it is critical that she feels valued and important. To achieve that, each employee who is a customer point of contact must be well trained in managing the customer experience, listening to them, communicating with them, and allowing them to feel as though they are the most important thing to that employee. And, at that moment, they should be. Two minutes later that employee may be working on something else and that's fine, but at the moment of interaction she must be totally with that customer. If a company can achieve that level of commitment to its customers, its customers will be just as committed to the company.

Customer Relationship Management

Question: Our ideal candidate will have a wealth of experience in customer relationship management, with a particular emphasis on developing new client relationships throughout the Fortune 500 market. Have you ever worked with Fortune 500 companies and, if so, how well did you perform?

Your Response: During my 8-year tenure with McKees Technology Systems, I was responsible for developing and managing customer service for all Fortune 500 and other key accounts throughout the Southeastern U.S. This included a great deal of customer interaction in relation to order specifications, product fulfillment, and ongoing technology support. My performance was consistently rated well above average for customer relationship management, customer service, problem solving, and project management. In fact, I received letters of appreciation from many of my accounts including Coca Cola, Home Depot, Boise Cascade, and others.

Customer Retention

Question: Now that we've got a great field team selling our products throughout the consumer market, we're looking at restaffing our customer service organization with professionals who understand how to manage and retain customer relationships. Can you address your experience in this area?

Your Response: I firmly believe that no sales or customer service organization is complete without equal emphasis on both selling and retaining customer accounts. With the ever-increasing cost of sales, it is essential that once a company has captured an account, it is able to service it and retain it for years to come. And, I'm pleased to say, that is my specialty! In fact, in each of my last three positions in customer service, I have been the individual selected to manage difficult customer relationships based largely on my success in solving problems, restoring confidence and retaining accounts. Prior to my arrival at my current company, our customer attrition was approaching 25%. Today, it's less than 7% and falling each quarter.

Customer Satisfaction

Question: Our company is currently ranked #1 in customer satisfaction in our industry. If we hire you, how can we be assured that your level of commitment to service and satisfaction is as strong as ours?

Your Response: That's easy. While employed as the Customer Service Manager for IBM's PC division, our customer satisfaction ranking improved from #5 to #2 in the industry. Then, under my leadership, Dell's customer satisfaction scores soared, from #8 to #1 in the home computer market. Most recently, I've taken a new technology company from virtual obscurity to #1 in the broadcast media market. I think these numbers speak for themselves and for my commitment to continually achieving #1 status.

Inbound Customer Service Operations

Question: The greatest challenge our inbound customer service center is facing is our constantly changing workforce. Because we employ young workers for an hourly wage, our HR department can't keep pace with the constant demands for hiring and training. Have you ever dealt with a similar situation?

Your Response: Fortunately, I've never been in the exact situation that you're describing. Although we've certainly experienced transition in our workforce, never has it been a monumental problem. I think that's largely because of the amount of time and effort we have devoted to hiring the right people and then ensuring that they are well-trained and supported. In fact, one of the recent projects I initiated was an employee reward and recognition system which provided our top performers with monetary incentives and retail discounts. It has been phenomenally well received and I anticipate it will be further expanded throughout the company.

Order Processing & Fulfillment

Question: When we created this new position, our primary goal was to put in place a system, a process, and personnel to expedite order processing and fulfillment. Can you relate any specific experience where you've successfully expedited these functions?

Your Response: Between 2001 and 2003, I worked with a team of customer service professionals responsible for the daily activities of Kodak's order processing and fulfillment center. It wasn't long after I joined the company that I began to notice some significant inefficiencies. It was easy for me to spot these since I was the first new hire in the department for more than four years. I began slowly, simply jotting down what I noticed and then, when appropriate, discussing it with my manager. Over time, as each of my recommendations was implemented, something wonderful happened. Orders were being processed and filled much faster than ever before, customers were delighted, and sales started to increase. Then, with full management support behind me, I launched a complete reorganization of the department, all technology systems, and all personnel. Now, I'm proud to say that we are processing and accurately filling orders at a rate 35% greater than when I arrived. I know I can do the same for you.

Outbound Customer Service Operations

Question: Tell me, step-by-step, how you would establish a new outbound customer service operation.

Your Response: I would begin with a clear definition of what the goals, responsibilities, and expectations of the operation would be. Following that, I would develop a strategic plan to guide the organization, a staffing and training plan to meet anticipated workload demand, a technology plan to facilitate the implementation of the appropriate technology tools and a tactical action plan defining all functions within the operation. Then, step-by-step, my team and I would start building the new organization, modifying our plans as necessary to meet the unexpected while working to achieve our operating goals. As each piece of the plan began to fit together, we would work cooperatively on integrating the next phase of the project. Never one to rush a major project or initiative, I am a firm believer in steady, progressive development, growth, and expansion.

Sales Administration

Question: Despite the fact that we're a small company, our sales administration function has grown substantially over the past several years. We're now looking at bringing in a Junior Administrator to work hand-in-hand with our Sales Administration Manager. Knowing that you've never worked in sales before, what skills do you bring to this position that make you qualified?

Your Response: You're right…I've never worked in a sales organization before. However, I have worked as an executive administrator for more than 10 years, during which time I have demonstrated outstanding organizational, project management, time management, and communication skills. In addition, I am able to quickly and accurately prioritize my workload to ensure that all deadlines and customer obligations are met. And, perhaps most important, I am trustworthy, capable of handling confidential information, and maintaining stringent ethical standards. Each of my past managers will attest to the quality of my performance and the strength of my character.

Service Quality

Question: Our current focus is on introducing and achieving stringent quality standards throughout both our sales and customer service organizations. Have you ever participated in any quality improvement projects with your current employer?

Your Response: Not only did I participate, I actually led a quality improvement initiative last year. Working in cooperation with outside quality consultants, and using ISO standards as our baseline measurements, my team and I implemented a series of quality improvements which impacted field sales, the sales contracting function, order processing, customer billing, and customer service operations. The best evidence of our success are the following stats: Sales have increased 22% in the past year, orders have increased 28%, fulfillment accuracy is at 42%, and customer satisfaction scores climbed from 78% to 95%.

KeyWord Accomplishment Phrases for Interviews, Resumes, & Cover Letters

Customer Communications

- Designed, wrote, and oversaw the production of a multimedia portfolio of customer communications, including print brochures, response mailers, radio and television advertisements, a user-friendly website, and a host of e-mail marketing messages targeting new bank customers nationwide.

Customer Loyalty

- Conceived and launched Wal-Mart's first-ever customer loyalty programs which rewarded buyers with a series of savings coupons and other incentives to halt encroaching competition and protect customer base.

Customer Relationship Management

- Honored as Pitney Bowes's "Customer Service Representative of the Year" for outstanding performance in customer relationship management within an intensely competitive regional market.

Customer Retention

- Halted losses through the introduction of an innovative customer retention program that far exceeded corporate objectives and retained better than 85% of core customer base despite relocation from Minneapolis to Detroit.

Customer Satisfaction

- Achieved and maintained a 95%+ customer satisfaction rating through expert performance in customer service, customer communications, problem solving, and order fulfillment.

Inbound Customer Service Operations

- Managed nationwide inbound customer service operations that processed over two million customer orders between November and December 2002, a 25% increase over the previous year.

Order Processing & Fulfillment

- Led warehouse staff of 45 who processed, filled, and shipped over 2,000 Dell computers each month for 18 consecutive months as the company's sales grew by more than 120% in 2002.

Outbound Customer Service Operations

- Recruited staff, established policies and procedures, and directed technology installation for the start-up of a regional outbound customer service operation marketing vacation and travel packages to consumers throughout the Northeastern U.S. Closed first year at 45% over sales and revenue goals.

Sales Administration

- Supported a 42-person field sales organization by efficiently and promptly handling all sales administration functions including order processing and fulfillment, customer correspondence and follow-up, problem research and resolution, field scheduling, and sales reporting.

Service Quality

- Benchmarked service quality initiatives for Motorola that reduced product failures by 12%, improved customer satisfaction 34%, and served as the model for all future Motorola quality and service programs worldwide.

Your Personal KeyWord Toolkit

Use the space below to add in KeyWords and KeyWord Phrases from your own career in Customer Service. Once you've done that, you'll want to do three more things essential to the success of your job search campaign.

1. Write KeyWord accomplishment phrases for each new KeyWord and KeyWord Phrase on your list. Then, use those words in your resume, cover letters, and interviews.

2. Write KeyWord interview responses to use when each of those KeyWord topics comes up. That way, you'll be instantly prepared with answers that effectively highlight your accomplishments, key projects, record of promotion, honors and awards, and other distinguishing aspects of your career.

3. Practice #1 and #2 above over and over! Although it certainly isn't necessary that you memorize each and every accomplishment and interview response, it is essential that the moment the topic comes up during an interview, you're immediately prepared to answer.

Your KeyWords & KeyWord Phrases:

_____

_____

_____

_____

_____

_____

_____

_____

_____

Chapter 7

KeyWords for the
Education Professional

Top 10 KeyWords & KeyWord Phrases

Academic Advisement
Classroom Management
Curriculum Design & Development
Educational Administration
Instructional Media
Instructional Programming
Scholastic Standards
Student Admissions & Retention
Student Services
Teaching & Training

KeyWord Interview Q&A

Academic Advisement

Question: At Roanoke, Virginia's first-ever magnet school, we've led the
academic community in the development of alternative educational programs for students of all ages. Our next project is the
creation of an academic advisement program for high school
students. Have you ever been involved in developing and/or
coordinating student academic advisement services?

Your Response: During my tenure as the Senior Guidance Counselor at Wilde
Lake High School in Columbia, Maryland, I led the task force
that established the school's first comprehensive academic ad-

visement programs for students planning to pursue both colle-
giate and vocational careers. Realizing that fewer and fewer
students stop their formal education after high school, it has
become apparent to educators nationwide that it is our responsibility to advise our students about the vast array of job and
career opportunities available to them through continued education. Over the course of two years, I created a stand-alone
academic advisement center with information and resources
from thousands of educational institutions nationwide. Last
year alone, we served over 1,000 students, and our program
continues to increase in popularity.

Classroom Management

Question: Consider the following scenario. You're a sixth-grade teacher
with 35 students, one of whom is continually disrupting your
classroom. Although you've spoken to the student on several
occasions and, most recently, discussed the situation with one
of the vice principals who, in turn, spoke to the student, the
situation continues to deteriorate. What would you do?

Your Response: Understanding that effective classroom management is critical
to student learning and retention, I would begin by calling in
the student's parents so that we could all discuss the situation.
At that point, I would outline acceptable classroom behaviors
and be sure that both the student and his parents completely
understood what was expected. I would also, in cooperation
with the parents, establish consequences for behaviors that were
unacceptable. If this did not alleviate the situation, I would have
no recourse but to withdraw the student temporarily from my
classroom and place in an individualized learning environment. As part of that student's IEP, I would develop a unit on
classroom behavior and expectations which would have to be
completed successfully prior to allowing the student to re-enter
my classroom. Further disruption would, unfortunately, result
in suspension.

Curriculum Design & Development

Question: We're most interested in your application because of your 10
years of experience in curriculum development. Please share
with the committee what you consider to be the most unique
curriculum you've developed and how you put it in place.

Your Response: Without a doubt, my greatest accomplishment in curriculum development was the creation of a hands-on technology program designed to teach students how to install, maintain, and repair local area networks. Completed in conjunction with our local vocational training center, I initiated the project with a comprehensive review of the networking industry, the latest technologies, and the most common applications. With that information in hand, I then created a 12-month training program, all classroom lectures and instructional tools, and a field internship program supported by our area's leading networking company. We launched the program in 1999, and over the past four years more than 300 students have graduated with their certificate in network repair.

Educational Administration

Question: Please outline for me the top three administrative qualifications you bring to the position of School Principal at Elmwood Middle.

Your Response: My top three qualifications all fall into the category of creative innovation - innovation in educational programming, in budget administration, and in teacher development and retention. As a Classroom Educator with more than 15 years' experience, I have demonstrated creativity and innovation in all facets of student learning, curriculum development, and instructional programming. As a Vice Principal with three years' experience, I have demonstrated my creativity in stretching budgeted dollars to their absolute limit to ensure that our teachers and our students had the educational tools and materials critical to their success. Finally, as a Trainer, I have taught, precepted, and mentored more than 20 student teachers throughout my career, all of whom I'm proud to say are still in the educational system.

Instructional Media

Question: Our recent push has been toward the development of instructional media and technology tools to supplement classroom teaching. What specific instructional media are you most familiar with?

Your Response: Having worked in some of the nation's poorest school districts in Appalachia, we've found ourselves feeling most fortunate just having enough textbooks for our students the vast majority of the time. However, realizing that if our students were truly going to succeed, we would have to better equip them to function in today's technology world, several teachers and I established the district's first-ever multimedia learning center. We began with a massive fundraising effort to solicit donations and refurbished technology; then set up a complete tech center with 20 PCs, all networked to the Internet, and a host of CD-based instructional and remedial learning programs. Now we are able to offer technology-based programs for all 260 students in our school as part of their regular classroom education.

Instructional Programming

Question: In my opinion, instructional programming is no longer just the traditional math, science and English curriculum. We are committed to furthering our course offerings and our student performance. Please highlight your experience in instructional programming to meet the needs of a diverse student body.

Your Response: To summarize, over the past five years, I have participated on educational programming committees that have led the state of Minnesota in innovative instruction and student learning opportunities. Most recently, we created a curriculum for HVAC repair and maintenance for our vo-tech students along with a two-year telecommunications training curriculum. Concurrently, for our students planning to enroll in college, we created several advanced placement programs in global navigation, bio-ethics, mortuary science, and philosophy. Our goal is to reach out to each and every student by offering innovative programs that meet his or her specific interests and occupational objectives.

Scholastic Standards

Question: Have you ever worked in a school system where students failed to meet scholastic standards and, if so, what was your response?

Your Response: I have been fortunate in my career because I've never been in that situation. I was, however, in a situation where scholastic standards changed abruptly when a new Board of Governors assumed leadership responsibility for our academy. When the other teachers and I returned after summer vacation, we were immediately faced with dramatic changes in what was expected of our students and the examinations they would have to pass in order to move to the next grade. Needless to say, it was a tremendously hectic period of time. Curricula were changed, new instructional materials were brought into the classrooms, an entire lecture series was developed to bring in additional expertise, and all existing tests were replaced with ones that more accurately reflected the information that students would be tested on at the end of the school year. It was a difficult year, yet we succeeded with more than 75% of our students meeting the new scholastic standards.

Student Admissions & Retention

Question: Over the past two years, we've been faced with a double-edged sword. Our admissions criteria have become much more stringent at the same time that our student retention numbers have dropped substantially. If you were given responsibility for solving this problem, what would you do?

Your Response: My first action would be to determine if the admissions criteria are indeed appropriate for the student body you are trying to attract and retain. Obviously, a great deal of thought went into your decision to stiffen the admissions criteria and I certainly would not want to question what's been previously determined to be appropriate. However, the academic climate has perhaps changed a bit and we may need to readdress each admission requirement. Regarding retention, the best place to start is with the student body. I would initiate a comprehensive project to collect and analyze data relative to why each student has left the University. Once compiled, this data should provide a wealth of knowledge about why retention is slipping and, in turn, provide the baseline we'll need to implement immediate and effective corrective actions.

Student Services

Question: We're most interested in a candidate who has experience in developing and directing student service programs. Can you address your experience in that arena?

Your Response: As the Director of Student Services for the University of Wisconsin, River Falls campus, I've spearheaded the start-up of a whole portfolio of student services in the areas of health care, off-campus housing, career development, on-campus employment, community service, athletics, and more. I believe that my responsibility is to ensure that all students have access to comprehensive service programs that will meet their needs and provide opportunities essential to the development of the whole student as they complete their undergraduate education.

Teaching & Training

Question: When I read your resume, I noticed that you'd had some experience in developing and delivering sales training programs for Pfizer's field sales team. Can you give me some details about that?

Your Response: Prior to my arrival at Pfizer, all sales training was provided by third-party consultants. I considered this a huge waste of money when it was obvious we had both sales and training talent in-house. I wrote a proposal outlining my recommendations and won full approval from the VP of Worldwide Sales to develop and deliver a six-part sales training program for all new hires. I carefully selected my training team from the company's sales and HR departments, and together we defined our learning objectives, created six individual program curricula, developed instructional tools and resources, and created supporting technology-based learning modules. We implemented the program within nine months and, to date, have trained more than 200 new sales representatives. It's been a phenomenal success and saved the company hundreds of thousands of dollars in training costs.

KeyWord Accomplishment Phrases for Interviews, Resumes, & Cover Letters

Academic Advisement

- Coordinated academic advisement for all 500 students enrolled in Notre Dame's Ecological Sciences major, including the start-up of the first-ever, on-campus recruitment programs for this new academic curriculum.

Classroom Management

- Honored as Forest Park's "Teacher of the Year" in 2003 for excellence in special education classroom management and student academic improvement.

Curriculum Design & Development

- Excelled in curriculum design and development for the theatrical arts, combining basic reading and math skills into each program to enhance student performance in all academic disciplines.

Educational Administration

- Promoted to Vice Principal after 12 years of classroom teaching to handle all educational and academic administration affairs for a 1,400-student high school with a staff of 89 teachers, 62 teaching assistants, and 15 support staff.

Instructional Media

- Pioneered the development and introduction of instructional media programs integrating the Internet, e-mail, database, word processing, and graphic arts technology to ensure that our students were well prepared for college admission and/or technical employment opportunities.

Instructional Programming

- Led two-year, city-wide, instructional programming initiative to upgrade science, mathematics, and technology curricula for 220 public schools serving Phoenix, Arizona.

Scholastic Standards

- Created the academic and instructional programs, selected the teaching staff, and led the way for San Diego's improvement from #10 to #2 in scholastic standards ratings in the state of California.

Student Admissions & Retention

- Introduced an entirely new operating infrastructure and improved the efficiency of the student admissions process by 24% while increasing student retention from 75% to 82%.

Student Services

- Expanded student services to include a monthly guest speakers program, biannual competitive sporting events, one-on-one and group peer counseling, and a campus-wide student newsletter.

Training

- Developed and taught a series of customer service and customer communication training programs for Bell Atlantic employees as part of the corporation's commitment to increasing customer responsiveness and improving customer retention.

Your Personal KeyWord Toolkit

Use the space below to add in KeyWords and KeyWord Phrases from your own career in Education. Once you've done that, you'll want to do three more things essential to the success of your job search campaign.

1. Write KeyWord accomplishment phrases for each new KeyWord and KeyWord Phrase on your list. Then, use those words in your resume, cover letters, and interviews.

2. Write KeyWord interview responses to use when each of those KeyWord topics comes up. That way, you'll be instantly prepared with answers that effectively highlight your accomplishments, key projects, record of promotion, honors and awards, and other distinguishing aspects of your career.

3. Practice #1 and #2 above over and over! Although it certainly isn't necessary that you memorize each and every accomplishment and interview response, it is essential that the moment the topic comes up during an interview, you're immediately prepared to answer.

Your KeyWords & KeyWord Phrases:

Chapter 8

KeyWords for
the Engineering Professional

Top 10 KeyWords & KeyWord Phrases

Capital Projects
Engineering Documentation
Process Development & Standardization
Product Development & Lifecycle Management
Project Management
Prototype Development
Quality Assurance & Management
Regulatory & Safety Compliance
Research & Development
Testing & Failure Analysis

KeyWord Interview Q&A

Capital Projects

Question: Now that we're planning a major expansion of our automotive
               plant, we're in need of a talented Project Manager with years of
               experience in capital projects. What have been some of the most
               notable projects that you've managed?

Your Response: Managing capital projects is what I do best and what I enjoy
               most. Here's a brief listing of some of my major projects: a $4
               million renovation to Saturn's manufacturing plant, a $9.8 mil-
               lion expansion of the Luxor complex in Las Vegas, a $2.3 mil-
               lion addition to IBM's corporate headquarters facility, and a $5
               million new construction project on behalf of AT&T. As you can

tell from the dollars involved, each of these was a major project involving hundreds of field personnel over a year or two time frame. What's most significant has been my financial success. Two of these projects were delivered within budget; one came in at $500,000 under budget, and the other at $1.8 million under budget. Considering the escalating costs of construction, these were notable achievements and the reason I've been personally selected to manage such large-scale capital projects.

Engineering Documentation

Question: Now that you've graduated, I assume you're interested in actually beginning your professional engineering career. Why should we consider you for a position in our engineering documentation department when we have so many other qualified entry-level candidates?

Your Response: First of all, Mr. Grunert will attest to the quality of my work performance during my internship in the engineering documentation department of your company. This five-month position gave me wide exposure to all the functions within the department, and I was able to establish good working relationships with everyone. So, most important, I'm not coming in as a total outsider. In addition, I have excellent organizational, oral and written communication, and project management skills, each of which I believe is important to the overall quality of work I will produce on behalf of the company. And, finally, I believe that the engineering documentation department is the place to start building my career. The opportunity will allow me to fully understand your products and technologies and then, hopefully, position me for a promotion to a position of even greater responsibility.

Process Development & Standardization

Question: Standardizing our work processes and engineering practices is one of the key milestones for our engineering group this year. What specific experience do you have that will support that initiative?

Your Response: Over the past two years, I have coordinated the effort to document and standardize all work processes for the R&D, product engineering, and industrial engineering departments at Black & Decker. This was a large project undertaken to not only standardize but also simplify our operations, realizing that there was excessive waste that we could eliminate and quality benchmarks we could achieve. The final work product we developed was more than 1,000 pages and clearly documented each and every work process within the departments we were studying. As a result, costs and waste have been reduced by better than 10%, the quality performance of these departments has met or exceeded all expectations, and the workforce has become much more stable. The latter was a by-product that we did not anticipate at the onset of our project, but quickly realized as soon as we provided a clearer road map for each employee to follow.

Product Development & Lifecycle Management

Question: I would like you to describe one of the products that you developed for McPherson's and how you managed that product throughout its lifecycle.

Your Response: The first product that comes to mind was a new line of upscale cutlery that I had designed. Several of our senior sales associates had brought the idea to the R&D department and assured us there was significant market demand. I was assigned lead responsibility for the project, from its initial design and engineering through testing to final manufacture. The entire project was completed in under nine months and our first full year of product sales grossed over $3.5 million. Realizing that the market did indeed exist, I then developed several auxiliary product lines and two years later managed a total redesign of the original product. Over the lifetime of the product, cumulative sales exceeded $50 million on an initial investment of only $1.8 million, quite a return on our efforts.

Project Management

Question: One of the most difficult tasks involved in managing multiple projects is appropriately managing time, personnel, equipment, and other resources to meet competing deadlines and demands. This is particularly true in an environment such as ours where we often have more than 20 projects under construction. As a Lead Project Engineer, how do you manage these conflicts?

Your Response: First and foremost, I work tirelessly at the front end of each project to carefully outline all the resource requirements that are needed and the timelines for each. By investing a bit more time at the onset of each project, I am able to immediately eliminate a number of issues through more efficient resource selection and scheduling. If a problem does arise, it becomes my sole responsibility to juggle those resources to ensure that all of our commitments are met, that our customers are satisfied, and that all projects are delivered on time. Scheduling, organization, and communication are vital to that function and some of the most valuable skill sets I bring to your company.

Prototype Development

Question: The new position that we are creating will focus almost exclusively on prototype development in our R&D laboratory. Although I see that you do have substantial R&D experience, I did not read anywhere on your resume that you've been responsible for prototype development. Have you?

Your Response: Inherent in my R&D responsibilities has always been the design and manufacture of prototypes for all new industrial equipment. In fact, it's one of the tasks that I most enjoy. I begin each project with a breakdown of all requisite personnel, technology, hardware, components, and other resources. Once that is complete, I assemble my team, establish the prototype development schedule, and oversee the actual construction and/or manufacture of the new equipment. I then coordinate all prototype testing, quality review and failure analysis functions, communicate those back to the engineering team, and then redesign our prototype to reflect those changes. Once this portion is complete, I write a final report documenting any other recommended design or engineering changes to further enhance the use and application of the equipment.

Quality Assurance & Management

Question: We're most interested in a candidate for our Quality Manager's position who has experience implementing ISO standards into other manufacturing organizations. Have you done this before and, if so, was it completed successfully?

Your Response: During my eight-year tenure with Nokia, I led the company's award of both ISO 9000 and ISO 14001 quality certifications at all 32 of their manufacturing facilities worldwide. Starting at the company's largest facility in Norway, I led the effort to receive certification, including the voluminous documentation requirements, and then followed through with step-by-step implementation. Once up and running, I then trained several of my key personnel to implement similar programs throughout our operations worldwide. This was a massive undertaking, but one that has clearly distinguished Nokia as the quality leader in the telecommunications industry.

Regulatory & Safety Compliance

Question: Regulatory affairs, safety compliance, OSHA requirements, and the like have become an increasingly large component of our engineering and manufacturing disciplines. What has been your specific experience in compliance-related issues?

Your Response: When I joined Pfizer's manufacturing management team, I knew that regulatory affairs would be a huge part of my responsibility. Yet, I had no idea of the complexity of working in an organization so tightly controlled and regulated as the pharmaceutical industry is. In my past positions with defense contractors, I thought I had dealt with as many regulations as possible. Defense doesn't even begin to compare with the pharmaceutical industry! As such, I've developed a unique expertise in implementing and monitoring compliance with state and federal regulations governing our operations and our safety practices. What's more important, I have met those demands and, in many instances, exceeded them. For the past four consecutive years, I have passed all regulatory audits with 100% compliance and no findings. What's more, I have reduced the number of safety violations by better than 70% and ended last year with no critical incidents. I am proud of my achievements for Pfizer and guarantee I can deliver the same strong results for your company.

Research & Development

Question: What is the single most significant R&D project you've ever worked on and what was the final outcome?

Your Response: Without a doubt, the most complex R&D project I've participated in was the development of Norton's original anti-virus software. Working in often uncharted waters as the concept of system viruses was relatively new, we were challenged to develop a new technology that would identify and eliminate viruses before we even knew what they were. In fact, to say that this project was complex is truly an understatement! Working in cooperation with a team of software and hardware engineers, and under the leadership of our project manager, we created something totally new and responsive to a need that only had begun to exist. Now, years later, Norton is the premier anti-virus software development company due, in large part, to our initial R&D efforts.

Testing & Failure Analysis

Question: Field testing and failure analysis of our next-generation track vehicles is one of the most important functions within our organization. How much related experience have you had?

Your Response: My military occupational specialty for the past several years has been in vehicular testing and performance analysis. As the prototype for each new track vehicle has been designed and built by Abrams, it has been shipped to our facility for extensive testing in mock combat situations. My teams and I put each vehicle through a rigorous, three-month evaluation where we field test every possible use and malfunction to determine the reliability of the design and the functionality of the vehicle itself. All systems are thoroughly checked and all failures clearly documented for redesign by Abrams's engineering team. Once a new vehicle has been completely tested and any redesign work completed, I am then responsible for the final sign-off and authorization for full-scale manufacture.

KeyWord Accomplishment Phrases for Interviews, Resumes, & Cover Letters

Capital Projects

- Managed $2.5 million in capital improvement and expansion projects in 2003. Delivered each project on time and under budget, saving the company $200,000 in expenses.

Engineering Documentation

- Automated the entire engineering documentation function, integrating engineering design, machine shop, and manufacturing operations into one consolidated engineering and project management system. Saved the company over $500,000 in annual personnel costs while significantly enhancing internal controls and project tracking capabilities.

Process Development & Standardization

- Spearheaded a $200,000 project to develop and standardize engineering processes for the design and prototype development of next-generation DVD technology projected for commercial market launch in 2005.

Product Development & Lifecycle Management

- As Product Manager, led the entire product development and lifecycle management function for Siemens's $450 million line of pacemaker batteries. Introduced eight new products over two years which generated an additional $50 million in annual revenues.

Project Management

- Managed a portfolio of facilities engineering and improvement projects as part of Maxell's commitment to creating a lean, quality-driven, cost-conscious manufacturing operation at all 12 of its facilities nationwide.

Prototype Development

- Spearheaded prototype development for all new video products in the engineering pipeline which, in 2003, were projected to generate $200 million in new revenues.

Quality Assurance

- Promoted from Quality Engineer to Quality Assurance Manager to lead the preparation and implementation of quality improvement initiatives to meet ISO 14000 requirements which we were awarded in 2002.

Regulatory & Safety Compliance

- Redesigned Merck's regulatory and safety compliance programs to meet more stringent federal requirements, passed all audit examinations, and retained all certifications with no audit findings.

Research & Development

- Member of eight-person R&D team which conceived and led development of alternative energy generation technologies to meet increased loads and user demands.

Testing & Failure Analysis

- Guided internal testing and failure analysis teams investigating catastrophic incidents of aircraft failure on behalf of NTSB's field investigation team. Demonstrated superb project management skills in stressful and time-sensitive situations requiring immediate information and action.

Your Personal KeyWord Toolkit

Use the space below to add in KeyWords and KeyWord Phrases from your own career in Engineering. Once you've done that, you'll want to do three more things essential to the success of your job search campaign.

1. Write KeyWord accomplishment phrases for each new KeyWord and KeyWord Phrase on your list. Then, use those words in your resume, cover letters, and interviews.

2. Write KeyWord interview responses to use when each of those KeyWord topics comes up. That way, you'll be instantly prepared with answers that effectively highlight your accomplishments, key projects, record of promotion, honors and awards, and other distinguishing aspects of your career.

3. Practice #1 and #2 above over and over! Although it certainly isn't necessary that you memorize each and every accomplishment and interview response, it is essential that the moment the topic comes up during an interview, you're immediately prepared to answer.

Your KeyWords & KeyWord Phrases:

_____

_____

_____

_____

_____

_____

_____

Chapter 9

KeyWords for the
Health Care Professional

Top 10 KeyWords & KeyWord Phrases

Acute, Chronic, & Ambulatory Care
Health Care Administration
Health Care Delivery Systems
Health Maintenance Organization
Managed Care
Patient Relations
Practice Management
Preferred Provider Organization
Risk Management
Third-Party Reimbursement

KeyWord Interview Q&A

Acute, Chronic, & Ambulatory Care

Question: I'm looking for a candidate who has worked in acute, chronic, and ambulatory care settings. Does your background include all three?

Your Response: Yes, I have experience in all three, but most significantly in acute and chronic care. As you probably read on my resume, most of my experience has been in emergency room and hospice nursing. When I joined the ER staff at Memorial Hospital, I found the environment stimulating, requiring me to think and act quickly in often life-threatening situations. During those four years, I also came to discover that I really enjoyed working with chronically ill patients who had presented in the ER with acute medical needs. It was at that time I accepted a nursing position with the LifeCare Center, a 120-bed hospice specializing in oncological care. It has been a wonderful experience and opportunity. Now, to briefly address my experience in ambulatory care, I did work one day a week for three years in the community health clinic adjacent to Memorial Hospital. This was also a great experience where I cared for a wide and diverse patient population presenting with every medical diagnosis you can imagine.

Health Care Administration

Question: What do you believe are the qualifications for excellence in health care administration?

Your Response: That's a huge question for which I'll try to give you a digestible answer. I believe the most talented health care administrators are successful because of the diversity of their talents in all general business disciplines - strategic planning, finance, budgeting, administration, human resources, technology, facilities, public affairs, and more. Unlike other business managers, a health care administrator must also be well trained in regulatory affairs, licensing, risk management, quality of care, and emergency preparedness to name just a few. Now, combine those diverse management tools with strong leadership, team building, problem solving, and communication skills, along with a dose of humanity, and you've got what I consider to be a talented health care administrator.

Health Care Delivery Systems

Question: Designing alternative health care delivery systems is one of our most critical functions. Unlike more traditional health care institutions, we lead the market in the innovation of care delivery models, quality of care practices, and holistic healing. What in your background demonstrates that you'll be successful in such a non-traditional environment?

Your Response: My personal commitment to holistic care is what interests me in your position and the reason why I know I'll be successful. s you know, all of my experience in radiology has been within the traditional hospital environment. However, because of my interest in treating the entire individual, I have taken six classes in alternative health care delivery and holistic healing, and completed a six-month volunteer internship at our local hospice. This was a particularly rewarding opportunity which allowed me to combine my radiological and medical skills with the expertise of other practitioners to create holistic treatment programs for patients throughout the facility. Now, at this point in my career, I am ready to transition into that type of environment on a full-time basis where I can be actively involved in developing alternative care systems, improving quality and caring for the entire human being.

Health Maintenance Organization

Question: Ten years ago, the health maintenance organization was a new model for health care delivery systems. It was revolutionary and was intended to change the entire industry. Unfortunately, expectations were not always realistic and we've learned that the HMO is not the answer. Bearing that in mind, what do you think can be done to fix the HMO model?

Your Response: My experiences with HMOs have been from one extreme to the other. I've seen some that work magnificently, are patient-centered, quality-centered, and cost effective. Conversely, I've also observed HMOs that somehow continued to operate in spite of themselves. As such, I'm not so sure that it's the model that needs fixing, but, rather, the structure and implementation of the HMO. When I observed these organizations, I noticed recurrent patterns in their specific operations that were key predictors of success or failure. Therefore, our challenge is to more clearly identify those success predictors and their underlying business systems and health care models. Once we understand those, we can reengineer the traditional HMO model and create the next-generation HMO that more accurately integrates the essentials of quality of care, cost of care, access to care, and the financial viability of the HMO itself.

Managed Care

Question: Marketing managed care services has become an increasingly complex and competitive activity. Years ago, we were the only health care company in the region to offer managed care programs to our corporate clients. Today, there are numerous other companies all vying for the same client base. As such, we need a top producer with a proven track record in this type of position. Tell me about your managed care sales experience and success.

Your Response: I began marketing managed care services in 1996 in the St. Louis market. At that time, managed care was a relatively new concept, and each sale required extensive negotiations to educate decision makers as to the relative merits and cost savings of managed care programs. I won the confidence of the local market and delivered revenues well beyond projections. I then accepted an assignment in Detroit, a well-established market with a great deal of competition. Within one year, I had closed three of the top five accounts in the market, virtually halting the growth of my competitors and dominating the market. Now, as Regional Market Manager for the upper Midwestern states, I have established our company as the premier managed care provider in the region, recruited and trained 10 outstanding sales producers, and closed over $120 million in sales last year.

Patient Relations

Question: Managing our patient relations department requires an individual with a host of talents, a tremendous amount of patience, excellent organizational skills, and the ability to communicate with patients, their families, and their care providers. What do you believe makes you qualified for this position since you've never worked in patient relations before?

Your Response: But, yes, I have worked in patient relations for years and years. As a Head Nurse, Nurse Supervisor, and Director of Nursing, managing patient relations has been an integral part of my job. Even as the DON, I still spend time with patients and their families to answer questions, provide information, recommend resources, and the like. I believe it is my responsibility to stay close to those we serve and not lock myself away in an office. What's more, because of my extensive nursing background, I am extremely well qualified to act as the liaison between physicians, surgeons, and specialty care providers, translating often complex information into terms that patients can understand. Needless to say, I also bring excellent organizational skills to your hospital, skills that I use on a daily basis as both nurse and administrator. I have found patient relations to be an area that not only do I enjoy, but in which I can have an extremely positive impact. As such, this is the foundation for my interest in this position and my guarantee to meet, if not exceed, all of your expectations.

Practice Management

Question: Moving from a Practice Manager for a small radiology practice into our practice management position with responsibility for six medical disciplines, 38 physicians, and more than 100 clinical and support staff is a huge leap in responsibility. Why should I believe you're prepared to handle so much?

Your Response: I can answer that quite simply. I'm prepared because I do have four years of practice management experience along with 12 years of experience working in a very large multidisciplinary practice much like yours. Although not the practice manager there, I did hold several supervisory positions with responsibility for people, projects, departments, and budgets. More importantly, I acquired substantial experience working in a large organization where coordination, communication, and documentation were the keys to success. Without a strong infrastructure to support the medical practice, the financial, business, and patient outcomes can be disastrous. Let me add that I left my position with the larger practice so that I could gain direct practice management experience which I now have. Thus, my goal is to now move back into a larger health care organization as its Practice Manager.

Preferred Provider Organization

Question: I've been asked by our Board of Directors to establish our first-ever preferred provider organization and I need a PPO expert to lead that project. Paul Kosinsky recommended you for the position and assured me that you were precisely the candidate we've been looking for. Why do you think that is?

Your Response: I've known Paul for about eight years now and worked closely with him at Charter Health Care when we set up our first PPO network. My responsibilities for this project varied widely and included identifying and negotiating with individual medical practitioners, and then conducting exhaustive reviews of their business and medical records. I worked closely with a team of attorneys to write the initial PPO agreement and several subsequent revisions, and actively participated in negotiations with each incoming practice. I consulted with our risk management team routinely while they established our formal policies and procedures, and did the same with the quality-of-care and cost-of-care teams. Paul and I were an excellent team, managing this project from concept to full-scale implementation in a little less than 18 months. Today, our PPO serves as a model for other provider networks nationwide.

Risk Management

Question: Controlling our risk exposure is more critical than ever before. As one of the region's most prominent hospitals, we are in a highly visible position within the health care community with the potential for extensive exposure. If we offer you the position of CFO for our institution, what steps will you take to reduce our potential risk?

Your Response: Obviously, the first step has to be a comprehensive review of the existing risk management policies, procedures and systems that you have in place. I cannot make any specific recommendations for change and improvement until I know what already exists. Once the review has been completed, I will then initiate a step-by-step plan to eliminate, or at a minimum reduce, the potential for risk exposure throughout the hospital. Let me add that this is a task that must be undertaken with the full support of all hospital personnel, from the maintenance staff to the surgical teams, and everyone in between. No risk management program or policy is any stronger than the individuals behind it. Therefore, as with other major projects I've spearheaded, this expansion of your risk management program must be a collaborative effort with buy-in from personnel throughout the institution.

Third-Party Reimbursement

Question: Our ability to collect third-party reimbursement has become even more difficult over the past several years. Now, with more than $600,000 in outstanding receivables, our practice is in need of an individual with the ability to work the system and accelerate reimbursement. What can you do to help us?

Your Response: Since resigning my position as the Practice Manager with a prominent cardiologist in Charleston, West Virginia, I've devoted the last three years of my career to working on a contractual basis with health care providers throughout the state to manage the recovery of their third-party reimbursement. Obviously, your practice is not the only one facing such stringent regulatory and documentation requirements. In years past, filing a claim was relatively straightforward. Today, it's a complicated process that requires expertise in the system and process, knowledge of specific entity requirements for timely filing, and the ability to build cooperative working relationships with personnel from various third-party payor organizations nationwide. This is the specific expertise I bring to you. Just last year alone, I recovered 80% of one practice's outstanding receivables; for another, 84%; and for another, 72%. I guarantee the same results for your practice.

KeyWord Accomplishment Phrases for Interviews, Resumes, & Cover Letters

Acute, Chronic & Ambulatory Care

- Acquired 5+ years' experience each in acute care, chronic care, and ambulatory care, clearly demonstrating my ability to quickly and effectively adapt to diverse health care organizations, environments, and patient care responsibilities.

Health Care Administration

- Appointed Administrator of a 245-bed tertiary care facility to orchestrate a complete turnaround, resolve long-standing quality-of-care issues, and halt financial losses. Within two years, achieved all objectives, restored profitability, restructured the entire quality function, and established Memorial Hospital as the leading health care facility in the region.

Health Care Delivery Systems

- Recognized for expertise in the design, development, and implementation of alternative health care delivery systems that have successfully augmented more traditional medical practices and resulted in double-digit gains in patient satisfaction.

Health Maintenance Organization

- Appointed to Kaiser Permanente's original management team that conceived, created, and launched the company's first-ever HMO, now the preferred model for health care delivery within the organization, and a $200 million revenue stream.

Managed Care

- Pioneered the concept of managed care as an alternative to the more traditional health care models used within the Centra Health organization, assembled team of health care administrators and practitioners to develop new model, and facilitated a two-year transition to become an entirely managed care organization.

Patient Relations

- Built and managed a unique, family-centered Patient Relations Department for a 150-bed hospice facility. Integrated patients, their families, medical practitioners, nursing practitioners, therapists, and all other parties into a holistic care organization dedicated to patient advocacy and quality of life.

Practice Management

- Founded the first-ever practice management association in the state of West Virginia, committed to transitioning the role and perception of the Medical Office Manager into that of the Practice Manager with broader management and decision-making responsibilities.

Preferred Provider Organization

- Created a preferred provider organization which encompassed all primary and secondary medical disciplines to create a single point of contact for all Yale University employees and their dependents. Significantly enhanced access to quality of care while reducing the University's health care costs by 8% annually.

Risk Management

- Retained the services of a leading health care consulting group to work with the hospital's legal staff in developing a more appropriate risk management program to further protect the institution from legal and/or financial exposure.

Third-Party Reimbursement

- Traveled throughout the region to assist independent medical practitioners in the preparation and filing of documentation for third-party reimbursement. To date, collected over $875,000 in outstanding receivables from both public and private sources and patients.

Your Personal KeyWord Toolkit

Use the space below to add in KeyWords and KeyWord Phrases from your own career in Health Care. Once you've done that, you'll want to do three more things essential to the success of your job search campaign.

1. Write KeyWord accomplishment phrases for each new KeyWord and KeyWord Phrase on your list. Then, use those words in your resume, cover letters, and interviews.

2. Write KeyWord interview responses to use when each of those KeyWord topics comes up. That way, you'll be instantly prepared with answers that effectively highlight your accomplishments, key projects, record of promotion, honors and awards, and other distinguishing aspects of your career.

3. Practice #1 and #2 above over and over! Although it certainly isn't necessary that you memorize each and every accomplishment and interview response, it is essential that the moment the topic comes up during an interview, you're immediately prepared to answer.

Your KeyWords & KeyWord Phrases:

_____

_____

_____

_____

_____

_____

_____

_____

_____

_____

Chapter 10

KeyWords for the Hospitality Professional

Top 10 KeyWords & KeyWord Phrases

Back-of-the-House
Catering & Convention Services
Facilities Management
Food & Beverage
Front-of-the-House
Guest Services
Labor Cost Controls
Menu Planning & Pricing
Multi-Unit Operations Management
Occupancy Management

KeyWord Interview Q&A

Back-of-the-House

Question: At Hyatt, we consider back-of-the-house operations as critical to the success of our properties as front-of-the-house operations. Guests may not see the kitchen, the housekeeping department, the maintenance department, or other operating areas, but they certainly see the results. Please take a minute to explain your strategy for managing back-of-the-house operations.

Your Response: First of all, I agree 100% with your comment. In fact, back-of-the-house operations are what allow the front end to work so smoothly and seem so effortless. And, in fact, that concept ties in specifically with how I build and manage my work teams. I want every employee who works for me to understand that he or she - individually - is making an impression on every single guest who enters our doors. Whether they're changing light bulbs, refreshing mini-bars, or installing a new building maintenance system, their input and the quality of the work reflects directly on the entire property. This team-based, quality-based management style is what has allowed my teams to consistently perform at their peak and, in fact, be honored for their accomplishments.

Catering & Convention Services

Question: As the premier conference center in Detroit, we're most interested in a candidate with a wealth of experience in selling catering and convention services. Can you detail your experience in this specialized sales field?

Your Response: As you've probably read on my resume, the vast majority of my experience with the Atlanta Conference Center has been in sales and new business development. A member of their 12-person national sales team, I traveled around the country to meet with prospective clients, attend association trade shows and expos, and call on the major associations in the DC metro area. Each year, for the past five years, I've closed a minimum of $1.6 million in convention sales, with one year topping $2 million. In addition, I also have substantial experience in on-site conference services which is, of course, of tremendous value in selling these services and ensuring client satisfaction. It was a wonderful experience in Atlanta and I was sorry to leave the city behind.

Facilities Management

Question: We're currently in the midst of a $25 million renovation to our hotel that will make our property the largest in the Milwaukee metro region. Needless to say, we're extremely excited about the project. Now that we're nearing completion, we're in the process of expanding our facilities management staff and are most interested in a candidate with substantial building and grounds experience. Can you address your specific experience during your impressive career with Omni?

Your Response: As you're aware, I began my career with Omni 12 years ago as a Maintenance Engineer. Since that time, I've earned six promotions based on my technical and management skills, and am currently the second-in-command of our entire facilities operation. Specifically, this includes all building systems, interior and exterior maintenance, and the entire 42 acres housing the property. Over the past two years, we've also managed an extensive renovation of rooms, common areas and all F&B outlets, along with a $6.9 million project to build an indoor tennis facility. That project, under my direct leadership, was delivered on time and within budget. In addition, I've been quite successful in retaining quality staff, thus eliminating a previous problem with constant employee turnover.

Food & Beverage

Question: Directing our food and beverage operations is a 24/7 job. Can you please describe the largest F&B department you've ever managed and your specific responsibilities?

Your Response: In my current position as F&B Director, I'm responsible for two full-service restaurants, a snack bar, and a 24-hour deli. Total staff averages a bit over 80 and total revenues from all four outlets exceed $8 million annually. With all that responsibility, I can assure you that I'm quite familiar managing in a 24/7 environment. Not only am I accustomed to working in this situation, I'm confident that I can deliver strong financial results as I've done in the past. Currently, our annual F&B revenues are up 17% over last year while our operating costs have been lowered by 10% through more efficient staffing, better training, improved vendor relationships, and a commitment to quality service.

Front-of-the-House

Question: Last year, our computer system crashed for two days and our front desk and reservations departments came to a virtual standstill. Revenues losses were significant and guests were extremely unhappy. What, if anything, could you do to ensure that never happens again?

Your Response: Although I certainly cannot assure you that there won't be any future technology problems, I can assure you that my staff would be trained to be proficient with our technology, yet equally proficient in manually processing all reservations, managing room assignments, generating guest bills, and the like. As technology has taken over virtually every facet of every business, a situation like you encountered reminds us that we must be able to operate the old-fashioned way - with paper, pen, and direct guest interaction. I can assure that under my leadership, your front-of-the-house operations would run smoothly and efficiently with or without technology tools.

Guest Services

Question: The reason we brought you in for an interview was based largely on your experience in guest services and guest relations. It is obvious that you have a wealth of experience in this area. Suppose, for example, that a major corporate client was dissatisfied with our service. How would you handle the situation?

Your Response: I can't imagine anyone would be dissatisfied with this property. It's magnificent and appears to be extremely well run. However, should that situation arise, my first step would be a face-to-face meeting with the corporate client to get a full description of what went wrong in his opinion and what we could do to restore his confidence in our property, our staff, and our service. Once that information had been collected and verified, corrective action would be immediately undertaken to ensure not only that client's satisfaction, but all others. One of the things I've learned after all these years in the industry is that if one client is unhappy, chances are the problem has also impacted other guests that we simply haven't heard from. The corporate client who spoke up is the one to be thanked for bringing any problems to our attention and allowing us to improve our operations.

Labor Cost Controls

Question: Tell me your greatest success in reducing labor costs and how that was accomplished.

Your Response: When I joined the management team at the Greenbrier, our labor costs in both the hotel and F&B operations were out of control. It was a problem that had plagued the property for years, and despite the best efforts of the previous management team, it continued to be a problem. Under my leadership, we more accurately defined our staffing and hiring requirements, implemented a series of in-house training and skills development programs, and launched an innovative staff incentive project that rewarded performance and longevity. Now, just 18 months later, our staff is stabilized and our labor costs are 15% under last year's. What's more, we're on track to further slash labor costs by an additional half million dollars a year and would anticipate achieving that goal by year-end 2004.

Menu Planning & Pricing

Question: If we offer you the position of Head Chef of our dining room, what can you do to expand our menu and reduce food costs?

Your Response: Since this is the first look I've taken at your menus, and because I'm not familiar with your actual food costs, it is obviously difficult for me to determine what specific steps I'd take. However, I can outline the process I would initiate. First and foremost would be a comprehensive review of the actual costs of each current menu item to ensure an acceptable profit margin. Where profits were not acceptable, an immediate remedy would be offered, either by increasing the menu pricing of the item or reducing associated vendor and preparation costs. Concurrently, I would also begin to introduce new menu items based on your specific customer demographics. All of these items would be accurately priced at the onset, so there would be no need for further review and analysis until a future date.

Multi-Unit Operations Management

Question: It's obvious from reading your resume that you have a strong background in the management of fast-food operations. However, this position requires managing six locations instead of just one. What makes you believe you're qualified to do this job?

Your Response: You're absolutely correct in your comment that I currently manage one single location. However, I also travel throughout the region to manage new restaurant openings, provide on-site training to newly hired management teams, and troubleshoot non-performing operations. This requires that not only can I manage the one location for which I have direct profit and loss responsibility, but that I can allocate my time and resources to meet the demands of the other locations under my leadership. I guarantee that taking operating and financial control of six locations is a position for which I am well prepared and in which I will succeed.

Occupancy Management

Question: Our occupancy numbers are dropping as a direct result of two new hotels that have opened in the immediate area. What, if anything, can you do to halt our losses and restore our occupancy levels to a consistent average of 85%?

Your Response: I believe that increasing occupancy requires a two-pronged approach. First, we must create the incentives to attract travelers to the property. This might include discounts for multiple-night bookings, a complimentary cocktail hour, partnerships with area attractions and restaurants, and a series of marketing campaigns that will distinguish this property from the others. In addition, equal emphasis must be placed on the quality of the guest experience - from the reservations department to the front desk, housekeeping, and parking garage. We want to create an environment where guests feel comfortable and where quality is consistently superior. Combine those two factors and your occupancy levels should rebound and stabilize.

KeyWord Accomplishment Phrases for Interviews, Resumes, & Cover Letters

Back-of-the-House

- Promoted to manage all back-of-the-house food service operations for the Luxor Casino in Las Vegas following the unexpected departure of the Operations Manager. Halted losses and restored profitability by renegotiating key vendor contracts, more effectively scheduling personnel, and introducing stringent portion controls.

Catering & Convention Services

- Coordinated all catering and convention services for Allstate's annual sales conference, an event hosting more than 2,000 people over a four-day period. Negotiated over $100,000 in event sponsors to deliver the first-ever conference with a bottom-line profit.

Facilities Management

- Managed facilities, capital improvements, and major construction projects for Sheraton Hotels in the Southeastern U.S. In the past year, directed a $2 million renovation in Charleston, a $1 million renovation in Key Biscayne, and a $25 million new hotel construction project in Charlotte, bringing all projects in on time and within budget.

Food & Beverage

- Sourced new vendors, negotiated contracts, and reduced food and beverage costs by 22% over six months.

Front-of-the-House

- Recruited and trained a 26-person, front-of-the-house staff for the grand re-opening of the exclusive Roosevelt Hotel in New York City.

Guest Services

- Introduced guest services, guest communications, and guest relations training programs for all front-of-the-house personnel. Resulted in a 24% increase in guest satisfaction ratings in spite of ongoing property renovation and associated guest inconveniences.

Labor Cost Controls

- Realigned staffing patterns and delivered over $100,000 in labor cost savings in the Facilities Management Department.

Menu Planning & Pricing

- Retained on a six-month contract to plan and price all new menus for Wendy's restaurants nationwide. Within six months of implementation, the company realized a 6% increase in bottom-line profitability on all food items.

Multi-Unit Operations Management

- Promoted from Restaurant Manager to Regional Manager to General Manager with full P&L responsibility for multi-unit operations throughout Kansas, Missouri, and Iowa, a $300 million region with 42 restaurants and 500-plus employees serving more than one million customers each year.

Occupancy Management

- Improved occupancy 23% at peak season and 14% the remainder of the year with no additional sales or marketing expenses.

Your Personal KeyWord Toolkit

Use the space on the next page to add in KeyWords and KeyWord Phrases from your own career in Hospitality. Once you've done that, you'll want to do three more things essential to the success of your job search campaign.

1. Write KeyWord accomplishment phrases for each new KeyWord and KeyWord Phrase on your list. Then, use those words in your resume, cover letters, and interviews.

2. Write KeyWord interview responses to use when each of those KeyWord topics comes up. That way, you'll be instantly prepared with answers that effectively highlight your accomplishments, key projects, record of promotion, honors and awards, and other distinguishing aspects of your career.

3. Practice #1 and #2 above over and over! Although it certainly isn't necessary that you memorize each and every accomplishment and interview response, it is essential that the moment the topic comes up during an interview, you're immediately prepared to answer.

Your KeyWords & KeyWord Phrases:

_____

_____

_____

_____

_____

_____

_____

_____

_____

_____

Chapter 11

KeyWords for the
Human Resources Professional

Top 10 KeyWords & KeyWord Phrases

Benefits Design & Administration
Diversity Management
Employee Communications
Employee Recognition
Employee Relations
Human Resources Information Systems
Labor Relations & Union Negotiations
Performance Appraisals & Promotions
Recruitment & Staffing
Training & Development

KeyWord Interview Q&A

Benefits Design & Administration

Question: One of the reasons that we attract such a high-quality workforce is the diversity of our employee benefits programs, among the best in the industry. Can you address your experience in benefits design and administration?

Your Response: Over the past 10 years, I have led and/or participated in the design, administration, expansion, improvement, and management of scores of employee benefit programs. These include, but are not limited to, health, dental, life and disability insurance, vacation, leave of absence programs and sabbaticals, employee assistance programs, employee communications, recognition and reward programs, an on-site child care facility, and a host of employee recreational and athletic programs. Most recently, I led efforts to introduce Digital's first-ever job-sharing initiative, which has been extremely well received by the workforce and already has several hundred participants within the first six months.

Diversity Management

Question: One of the most important commitments we have made to the community and the local economic development commission is to recruit a diverse workforce which accurately reflects the composition of the local population. What do you consider to be the two or three most critical factors in attracting and retaining these employees?

Your Response: First and foremost, creating the right culture is essential. Not only must you attract these employees, you must create an environment that welcomes them by educating your existing workforce. Just as important, you must create the right training programs so that these new employees can quickly and effectively assimilate into the company. Third, you must establish an open environment that is responsive to these employees and their ideas to ensure that they feel they are a part of the company and not just an addition. And, finally, I would also encourage the design of employee benefit programs that closely align with the specific needs of these diverse populations.

Employee Communications

Question: Do you have any direct experience in writing and designing employee communications?

Your Response: One of my first positions with IBM was in their Employee Services Department where I was directly responsible for writing the monthly newsletter distributed to employees worldwide, coordinating quarterly management-employee brainstorming meetings to facilitate information sharing, and writing all supporting employee documentation when benefit programs were added, expanded, and/or deleted. In fact, employee communications is one of the areas I most enjoy, allowing me to combine my HR expertise with my strong writing skills. Even as Assistant HR Director today, I continue to write articles for the employee newsletter on a regular basis.

Employee Recognition

Question: The upper management team is currently evaluating the feasibility of adding employee recognition programs, something that we've never done in the past. As a small company committed to controlling our costs, we felt that recognition programs would be too costly in addition to all the other benefits we currently fund. If we offered you the position, would you be able to establish such a program?

Your Response: First of all, let me share with you that employee recognition programs do not have to be expensive. In fact, some of the best programs my colleagues and I have ever formulated cost my employer almost nothing. For example, we recently created a sales recognition program to reward top producers. With a little creative thought and marketing, we were able to obtain 100% program funding through a partnership with RSSC, the parent company of Royal Caribbean Cruise Lines. Last year, we wanted to reward our top administrators and support staff with a small gift. Instead of working with one of the major corporate gift suppliers, we found a local company who supplied the gifts at 40% less. Simply put, recognition programs are all about recognition and not the dollars spent.

Employee Relations

Question: With the unionization of our manufacturing workforce, we've begun to encounter some difficult situations between union and non-union personnel. Will you be able to offer any solutions to us to strengthen our employee relations programs and, in turn, employee cooperation?

Your Response: Effectively managing employee relations boils down to one key factor - communication. It is essential that diverse workforces have a forum through which they can communicate easily and safely with one another, sharing concerns, brainstorming solutions and working for the mutual benefit of the company. I've found in my past experiences that top management should, whenever possible, stay out of these situations and allow the employees and their line managers to build the communication channels that will allow for positive working relationships and cooperation.

Human Resources Information Systems

Question: Our primary objective in this current search is to identify a candidate with a strong combination of both HR and technology experience. Are you that candidate?

Your Response: Yes, without a doubt, I am that candidate. I began my professional career as a Programmer with IBM, specializing in the design and delivery of customized HRIS solutions for Fortune 500 clients. Over the years, I earned several promotions to my final assignment with them as the Director of HRIS. I then accepted an opportunity with a technology-based venture capital group where I have continued to spearhead the development of state-of-the-art HRIS software and hardware solutions. It is what I do best and it is the greatest value I bring to your organization.

Labor Relations & Union Negotiations

Question: I have to be honest and tell you that our union has really been beating us up lately. No matter the concessions we offer, it seems as though they're never satisfied. It has been extremely frustrating. As such, we're looking for a candidate who can take control and restore stability. What has been your experience is such situations?

Your Response: Although my colleagues can never understand why, I thoroughly enjoy the challenge of union negotiations and labor relations. And a challenge it can often be as you've described. However, as committed as you are to your company, the union is just as committed to their workforce which, as we all know, is one of the most vital components for the success of any organization. My contribution in these situations has been to establish channels for open communication and build cooperative working relationships. By doing so, when a difficult situation arises and the company cannot meet union demands, both sides enter the negotiating room ready to talk and ready to solve the issue at hand. What's more, I have a winning track record in negotiating grievances to the benefit of both parties while protecting the integrity and financial viability of the company.

Performance Appraisals & Promotions

Question: Why, after so many years in sales management, would you want to consider a position managing the performance appraisal and promotion system within our HR department? We're having a difficult time understanding why you're interested in making such an abrupt career change.

Your Response: My answer to that question is really twofold. First of all, throughout my sales career I have been directly responsible for performance appraisals and promotions for a sales team of up to 200 individuals. I have found this to be a particularly rewarding facet of my management responsibility and one that I take quite seriously. Having the opportunity to help younger professionals plan and develop their careers is a wonderful contribution to make to the success of any organization. Secondly, and on a personal note, I would like to return to San Diego and establish my new base here. After more than 20 years of living on the road and in hotels, I'm ready to live at home.

Recruitment & Staffing

Question: Now that our new agricultural production facility is nearing completion, we're in an aggressive recruitment and staffing phase. However, so many people have left our rural community to move closer to Chicago, that we're having a difficult time attracting qualified personnel from the local market. What suggestions can you offer to help us solve this problem?

Your Response: I think your first step has to be becoming more visible within the local community. As a native of the area, I hear so many people talking about the big construction project down on Route 47, but few know much about this company and its outstanding reputation in the industry. I would begin with a full-scale marketing blitz announcing the projected grand opening and encouraging early employment opportunities. I would closely network with the local employment assistance offices and employment agencies, and would host several on-site job fairs. Obviously, consideration will also need to be given to attracting personnel, primarily supervisory and management level, from larger markets in Illinois and surrounding states. Although relocation costs must be kept to a minimum, it is critical to recruit and staff the organization with the right people from the beginning. A bit more invested at the onset will help eliminate future restaffing costs.

Training & Development

Question: We need a top-notch training and development expert in this position. Why should we consider your candidacy?

Your Response: I can answer that question in three easy sentences. First, I have been in corporate training and development for the past 12 years with Johnson & Johnson, Merck, and Bayer. Second, I have coordinated the development of more than 200 new training programs in the areas of sales, customer relationship management, finance, administration, technology, and HR administration. Third, three of the programs I have developed have been honored by the American Society of Training and Development for innovation and excellence. As such, it is readily apparent that I have the scope and depth of experience you are seeking and that much of that experience has been on the leading edge of corporate training.

KeyWord Accomplishment Phrases for Interviews, Resumes, & Cover Letters

Benefits Design & Administration

- Redesigned all benefits programs and administered their implementation as Rexall introduced an entirely new portfolio of health care, dental care, employee assistance, life insurance, disability insurance, leave of absence, and academic reimbursement programs for all 12,000 employees worldwide.

Diversity Management

- Championed development and implementation of a series of diversity management programs involving recruitment and hiring, training, and promotion. Honored as Cincinnati's "best employer" in the categories of both diversity management and community outreach.

Employee Communications

- Authored a series of employee communication programs to halt workforce tension and instability resulting from the firm's massive layoff in 2003. Restored employee confidence in the company and its long-term viability within the industry.

Employee Recognition

- Managed annual employee recognition and awards programs for IBM's global sales organization, upgraded the quality of the recognition honors, and publicized each individual employee and his corporate contributions.

Employee Relations

- Introduced a number of employee relations initiatives to enhance the relationships between employees and management, eliminate unnecessary grievances, and better communicate the economic value of the workforce to the community, corporate leaders, and local politicians.

Human Resource Information Systems

- Spearheaded the introduction of next-generation HRIS technology, valued at $400,000, to keep pace with the changing needs of both the corporation and its employees.

Labor Relations & Union Negotiations

- Managed labor relations and negotiations with two separate unions representing the 20,000-employee workforce at General Motors. During my eight-year tenure, plants never experienced work stoppages resulting from union actions and I successfully arbitrated scores of employee grievances, all to the company's benefit and with union support.

Performance Appraisals & Promotions

- Redesigned performance appraisal and promotion system to more accurately identify top producers and contributors to the company, eliminate nepotism, and ensure that the workforce remained stable despite the economic downturn.

Recruitment & Staffing

- Spearheaded a massive recruitment and staffing initiative that brought an additional 250 telemarketers into the organization to manage the nationwide launch of Bank of America's Customer Care Program.

Training & Development

- In 2003, developed and introduced 14 new employee training and development programs for personnel throughout the company's finance, accounting, IT, and purchasing organizations. Net result of training has been a measurable improvement in employee productivity and retention.

Your Personal KeyWord Toolkit

Use the space below to add in KeyWords and KeyWord Phrases from your own career in Human Resources. Once you've done that, you'll want to do three more things essential to the success of your job search campaign.

1. Write KeyWord accomplishment phrases for each new KeyWord and KeyWord Phrase on your list. Then, use those words in your resume, cover letters, and interviews.

2. Write KeyWord interview responses to use when each of those KeyWord topics comes up. That way, you'll be instantly prepared with answers that effectively highlight your accomplishments, key projects, record of promotion, honors and awards, and other distinguishing aspects of your career.

3. Practice #1 and #2 above over and over! Although it certainly isn't necessary that you memorize each and every accomplishment and interview response, it is essential that the moment the topic comes up during an interview, you're immediately prepared to answer.

Your KeyWords & KeyWord Phrases:

_____

_____

_____

_____

_____

_____

_____

_____

_____

_____

Chapter 12

KeyWords for the Human Services Professional

Top 10 KeyWords & KeyWord Phrases

Behavior Management & Modification
Case Management
Client Advocacy
Counseling
Crisis Intervention
Diagnostic Assessment & Evaluation
Discharge Planning
Program Planning & Administration
Social Services
Treatment Planning

KeyWord Interview Q&A

Behavior Management & Modification

Question: One of the things that intrigued me most about your background was your extensive involvement in the development of behavior management and modification programs. Can you elaborate on this?

Your Response: As a special education teacher, managing the classroom is one of my greatest challenges. With an average of 15-18 students in my room each day, each at a different educational level, each with unique physical and psychological problems, it is imperative that I maintain an orderly and motivating learning environment. Early in my career, I learned that one of the best ways to achieve this was to create and implement customized behavior management programs for each and every student. If I was able to manage their behavior in the classroom, work to eliminate unacceptable behaviors through various behavior mod and reward systems, then I would be much more effective as a teacher. Undoubtedly, this has been the case as my teacher ratings have been consistently superior and my students' performance well above average for such a diverse special needs population.

Case Management

Question: What is the largest-ever caseload you've managed and what was the composition of your clients?

Your Response: While employed as a Social Worker with the Idaho Department of Social Services, I managed a caseload that averaged about 80 children. All of these children had been taken from their homes because of alleged abuse and had been placed under protective care with the state. To be honest, it was much too large for any individual because of the complexity of the caseload and the vast number of parties involved in each child's care and placement. However, I was able to meet all of my obligations and provide the quality of care and case management so vital to these children.

Client Advocacy

Question: Advocating on behalf of our nation's youth and, in particular, their need for full health coverage regardless of socioeconomic status is the primary mission of this agency. Knowing that you've worked in various social service and human service organizations throughout your career, I assume you have experience in client advocacy. What specifically is that experience?

Your Response: I consider client advocacy to be the foundation on which my entire professional career has been built. Regardless of the specific population I was serving at any moment in time, my responsibilities have always entailed working as an advocate on their behalf to facilitate and expand service delivery, acquire funding, develop new programs, expand staffing competencies, and represent their interests before state and federal legislators. In fact, last year I spoke before the National Commission on Youth Services to provide statistical data on health care coverage and accessibility. The year before, I presented at the American Medical Association in an effort to expand the volunteerism efforts of health care providers nationwide. I believe that it is my responsibility to advocate for my clients and do everything in my power to enhance their quality of life.

Counseling

Question: Please describe your specific approach for counseling inmates prior to their release.

Your Response: I believe that effective counseling programs result from a combination of three primary factors. First, a counselor must be well trained and well educated in the theories and practical applications of counseling. I have met this requirement through a wealth of educational experiences, highlighted by a master's degree in counseling. Second, a counselor must be flexible in meeting the needs of her specific client base. Obviously, this is a unique consideration when working with an incarcerated population, many of whom have been imprisoned for 10, 15, or more years. As such, my counseling programs are designed to respond to their unique needs for assimilating back into society. Third, and perhaps most important, each client I counsel must be motivated. If they are not, then it's virtually impossible to provide the depth of counseling and support that will ensure their success once they've left the prison. I've been particular effective in this area and currently have a recidivism rate lower than 15%.

Crisis Intervention

Question: Please describe your protocol for crisis intervention.

Your Response: As a Crisis Hotline Counselor for the past 12 years, I've personally dealt with a vast array of crisis situations ranging from suicides and other self-injurious actions to terrorist incidents and the resulting crises that arose. I pride myself on my ability to remain calm in any situation, enlist the support of other personnel and agencies as appropriate, and handle each call in a professional and responsive manner. My protocol is straightforward. I begin with an immediate assessment of the situation, work to open channels of communication with the caller, and provide the support needed at that particular moment to handle the crisis at hand. Then I create a follow-up plan to provide ongoing intervention as may be needed.

Diagnostic Assessment & Evaluation

Question: Accurately diagnosing incoming patients is more critical than ever before, particularly considering our shrinking personnel and financial resources at the psychiatric facility. As such, we are most interested in a candidate with a wealth of experience in diagnostic assessment along with the ability to manage this function efficiently and with minimal support resources. Does your experience support that?

Your Response: Throughout my career, whether working in an inpatient or out-patient psychiatric facility, I have independently managed the entire diagnostic assessment and evaluation process for all incoming geriatric clients. This can be a particularly challenging population to work with since many present with a variety of physical ailments unrelated to their psychiatric condition, but nevertheless, impacting their capabilities. As such, I use a two-pronged approach to diagnostic assessment which integrates psychiatric needs with physical needs. Using a combination of both client interviews and documentation from past care providers, I am generally able to quickly grasp the specific needs of each client, clearly diagnose his conditions, and facilitate the development of appropriate care and intervention programs.

Discharge Planning

Question: We've created this new position in an effort to standardize our discharge planning protocols and improve patient follow-up. Why do you consider yourself qualified for this assignment?

Your Response: Discharge planning has been an ongoing responsibility of mine since coming to St. Mary's Psychiatric Hospital in 1998. Currently, I work with a team of other care providers - a psychiatrist, a psychologist, two nurse practitioners, and two counselors - to develop individualized discharge plans for each and every one of our patients. My role has been to facilitate this group, coordinate service delivery with community-based mental health facilities and practitioners, and implement follow-up programs to ensure that each patient is meeting his or her obligations and continues on the path to recovery and independent living. I thoroughly enjoy this function and would be delighted to have the opportunity to coordinate discharge planning on a full-time basis for patients throughout your facility.

Program Planning & Administration

Question: In finding the right candidate for this position, we'd like to know more about your experience in program planning and administration.

Your Response: As the Director of Community Outreach, one of my primary responsibilities is the identification of client needs and the subsequent development, implementation, and management of responsive programs. Over the past five years, I've introduced more than 20 different programs ranging from group and individual counseling to community-sponsored fundraisers to client advocacy and more. I believe that the combination of my skills in strategic planning, project management, organization, communication, and budgeting have been critical to my success in this function and will continue to serve my agencies well throughout my career.

Social Services

Question: In reviewing your resume, it is apparent that you have never worked in a social service environment before. Why your interest at this point in your career?

Your Response: You're right in assuming that my entire background has been as a human resources professional in the corporate world. However, much of my experience has been in the development and delivery of employee assistance programs and, more specifically, in employee counseling. The reasons for counseling have run the gamut from workplace-related problems to a host of personal issues involving marriage, children, finances, health, and both psychiatric and emotional problems. The latter is where I have really excelled and the reason for my current change in career direction. I have found the greatest personal rewards in my ability to counsel employees through difficult personal situations, intervene appropriately in crisis situations, and reach out to the local community for additional resources as necessary. In fact, just last year, I worked with Lisa Libon of your agency to coordinate service delivery for one of our employees. As such, I am somewhat familiar with how your agency operates, the resources at your disposal, and your commitment to quality care and intervention.

Treatment Planning

Question: One of the primary responsibilities of this position is to develop treatment plans for each client admitted to our halfway house. Have you ever been responsible for treatment planning and, if so, for what types of populations?

Your Response: As a nurse practitioner with more than 15 years of experience working in psychiatric hospitals, prisons and other residential facilities, I bring a wealth of knowledge in treatment planning. In fact, one of the most rewarding facets of my career has been to develop plans, either participate in or observe their implementation, and then, hopefully, see the fruits of our labor as clients are discharged and thrive within their local communities. Perhaps most important to that process is the collaboration among the various care providers, each working to contribute his expertise in formulating a holistic approach to care, treatment, and successful intervention.

KeyWord Accomplishment Phrases for Interviews, Resumes, & Cover Letters

Behavior Management & Modification

- Specialized in the development and delivery of customized behavior management and modification programs for children diagnosed with a series of emotional and psychological conditions as part of the state's mandated special education programming requirements.

Case Management

- Managed a caseload of more than 100 parolees previously convicted of drug- and alcohol-related criminal activity. Despite huge caseload and documentation requirements, consistently maintained schedules, appointments, and all follow-up obligations.

Client Advocacy

- Created Minnesota's Client Advocacy Awareness Project, a key component in the state's commitment to successfully integrating non-violent patients from various mental health facilities back into the community with the community's support and cooperation.

Counseling

- Graduated with top honors from McGrath University with a Ph.D. in Child Counseling and dual minors in Group Dynamics and Human Services Administration.

Crisis Intervention

- Trained and supported a team of 50 crisis intervention counselors providing immediate care to clients presenting with a host of self-violent behaviors and actions. Successfully halted more than 35 suicide attempts over the past year.

Diagnostic Assessment & Evaluation

- Created a portfolio of diagnostic assessment and evaluation tools which more accurately identified schizophrenic and psychotic behaviors prior to full-scale onset.

Discharge Planning

- Personally handled discharge planning for all patients transitioning from lock-down facility into community-based housing. Coordinated discharge planning with medical, psychiatric, therapeutic, and legal personnel assigned to each patient to ensure compliance and patient success.

Program Planning & Administration

- Honored with the 2003 "Administrator of the Year" award from Shepherd Pratt Hospital for expertise in program planning, administration, and innovation. Rolled out more than 25 new patient care, patient counseling, and staff development programs during three-year appointment as the facility's Administrator-in-Charge.

Social Services

- Appointed to Governor's Task Force for the complete redesign of all social services programs, agencies, and operations throughout the state of Wyoming. Initiative impacted more than 400,000 residents consuming the services of more than 100 community-based agencies staffed by hundreds of professionals and support personnel.

Treatment Planning

- Directed treatment planning and intervention for all newly admitted patients to the LifeCare long-term hospital and hospice complex in Detroit. Position required constant interactions with department managers throughout the facility to ensure the immediate implementation of treatment plans, medications, and emergency interventions.

Your Personal KeyWord Toolkit

Use the space below to add in KeyWords and KeyWord Phrases from your own career in Human Services. Once you've done that, you'll want to do three more things essential to the success of your job search campaign.

1. Write KeyWord accomplishment phrases for each new KeyWord and KeyWord Phrase on your list. Then, use those words in your resume, cover letters, and interviews.

2. Write KeyWord interview responses to use when each of those KeyWord topics comes up. That way, you'll be instantly prepared with answers that effectively highlight your accomplishments, key projects, record of promotion, honors and awards, and other distinguishing aspects of your career.

3. Practice #1 and #2 above over and over! Although it certainly isn't necessary that you memorize each and every accomplishment and interview response, it is essential that the moment the topic comes up during an interview, you're immediately prepared to answer.

Your KeyWords & KeyWord Phrases:

_____

_____

_____

_____

_____

_____

_____

_____

_____

Chapter 13

KeyWords for the International Business Professional

Top 10 KeyWords & KeyWord Phrases

Cross-Border Transactions
Cross-Cultural Business Relations
Foreign Government Relations
Global Business Development
Import & Export Operations
International Trade
Joint Venture Transactions
Mergers & Acquisitions
Multinational Contract Negotiations
Worldwide Sales & Marketing

KeyWord Interview Q&A

Cross-Border Transactions

Question: Negotiating cross-border transactions is one of the most critical functions of this position. Can you detail your experience in structuring and negotiating those types of transactions?

Your Response: Throughout my career with Eastman Kodak, I have led a number of cross-border transactions. Specifically, I've structured, negotiated, and closed cross-border sales, joint venture and strategic alliances with companies throughout Mexico. Our cross-border sales programs have led to an additional $40-plus million in annual sales, our cross-border joint ventures have provided Kodak with well-established market presence in both Mexico City and Cancun, and our cross-border strategic alliances have dramatically expanded our third-party distribution network throughout the country.

Cross-Cultural Business Relations

Question: In reviewing your resume, all of your experience appears to be within the U.S. With that said, why do you think you would perform well in a position where a great deal of your responsibility would be cross-cultural business relations and account management?

Your Response: You're right...my experience has all been within U.S. markets. However, the diversity of that experience is where I have best demonstrated my ability to negotiate, close, and retain customer accounts. For example, imagine how different the presentation and negotiation styles are when dealing with the U.S. government as compared to a privately owned construction company. Or a Fortune 500 company with scores of individuals involved in each transaction as compared to a venture capital fund with only two partners. It is this diversity that is my greatest value. It is my ability to quickly build rapport with virtually any potential customer. It is my success in understanding each and every customer's need and then delivering on what I have promised. I will be just as successful with your customers, whether in the U.S. or abroad.

Foreign Government Relations

Question: Managing relationships and negotiations with foreign government officials can often be a difficult assignment. On your resume, you briefly highlighted a project in which you negotiated directly with government personnel in India. Can you please elaborate on this for us?

Your Response: In the summer of 2001, Georgia Pacific began to look at building a manufacturing facility in southern India. A team of professionals with experience in international business development was formed, and I was selected to head up government affairs for the project. Over the next 14 months, I traveled back and forth between the U.S. and India, first working to establish GP's initial government contacts, and then devoting hundreds of hours to developing those relationships and gaining the

government's support for our project. There really are no words
to describe the enormity of the task. In total, I negotiated with
representatives from more than 15 different government agencies, each with his own regulations and each with his own
agenda. Now, three years later, the project is about 80% complete, with plant start-up scheduled for mid-2005.

Global Business Development

Question: Please detail any experience you have in global business development, both strategy and execution.

Your Response: In my current position as a Senior Marketing Strategist for Allied Chemical, my principal responsibility is the research, col-
lection, analysis, and delivery of business intelligence to guide
the company's internal growth and expansion. To date, I've
participated in projects supporting development of Allied operations in Nigeria, Ghana, Qatar, and Venezuela. When these
projects are complete, it is projected that each will generate revenues in excess of $15 million annually. Perhaps even more
important, I provided information that was essential to halting
a project under consideration in Saudi Arabia several years ago,
believing the market to be too unstable and unpredictable. The
losses Allied would have sustained, had this project proceeded,
would have been enormous.

Import & Export Operations

Question: Our import and export departments are in need of a complete
overhaul. As we've grown so quickly over the past five years,
some of our internal operations haven't kept pace. Do you think
that you can help with this situation?

Your Response: I know I can help! The business of importing and exporting
becomes more and more complex with each passing year and, if
you don't keep pace, you're bound to get lost in the maze of
regulations and documentation. I guarantee that I can come
into your organization, quickly gain control of the operation,
implement changes as necessary, upgrade technology resources
to meet demand, and regain regulatory compliance. Just give me
six to nine months, and you'll be amazed at the results.

International Trade

Question: We're just in the process of expanding our domestic trade operations into several key international markets. As such, we're most interested in a candidate with international trade experience. Has this been a function for which you've been responsible?

Your Response: Throughout my legal career, I've consulted with corporate clients on a host of issues pertinent to international trade and international business transactions. Working on behalf of U.S. companies in the petrochemical, utility, and construction industries, I've structured and negotiated more than 50 international sales, joint venture, and acquisition contracts. In fact, these transactions have been the most interesting work I've done in my career. I thoroughly enjoy the challenge of international negotiations and the opportunity to work with such a diversity of business and legal professionals. The only reason I am considering another opportunity is that your position would allow me to function entirely within an international market.

Joint Venture Transactions

Question: We're in the midst of a complex joint venture with Exxon for the development and construction of a massive refinery project in Nigeria. What, if any, joint venture experience do you have?

Your Response: Most recently, I worked on a six-person team that structured and closed a JV between my company and a small co-generation facility in New England. This was a critical project which has now provided us with our first-ever presence within that market. My role in the JV included comprehensive review of our JV partner's financial performance over the past 10 years and financial consultation with the legal team drafting the actual JV agreement. In addition, I sat in on negotiations to provide financial interpretation of specific details as necessary and to ensure full financial disclosure by all parties.

Mergers & Acquisitions

Question: How many merger and acquisition transactions have you been involved with over the past three years?

Your Response: When I joined the Russian Economic Development Venture Group in 2001, I was hired specifically to manage their M&A

activity throughout all former Soviet Union countries. Our mission was twofold: First, we wanted to quickly identify and evaluate potential merger opportunities with what we considered to be leading-edge firms poised for substantial growth both within their specific countries and worldwide. Second, we wanted to identify and execute several substantial acquisitions. Working in cooperation with two other M&A experts, several attorneys, and local government officials, I immersed myself within the business communities of each country we had targeted and began the process of identifying potential partners. As you can imagine, negotiations were often difficult and the red tape was unbelievable, yet we succeeded. To date, we've acquired two industrial equipment companies and four consumer product companies for a total investment of more than $25 million. In addition, we've structured and negotiated a dozen mergers that are projected to generate combined annual revenues of more than $150 million over the next five years.

Multinational Contract Negotiations

Question: Often the most difficult negotiations are those with our multinational clients because of their diverse product needs to meet their broad market reach. Please detail your most complex multinational contract negotiation, the players, the challenges, and the results.

Your Response: Undoubtedly, the single most difficult contract I've ever negotiated was a $35.5 million contract with Siemens for the sale of digital photographic technologies. To begin with, the number of players involved in the contract was phenomenal. Representing Siemens, there were four senior executives, each from a different country in Europe, more than 10 attorneys, two senior financial analysts, two European-based World Bank representatives, and six purchasing managers. Then, although all negotiations were conducted in English, there were several translators required to ensure that all non-native English-speaking executives clearly and completely understood the contract negotiations. Our only major obstacles to overcome during negotiations pertained primarily to scheduling and shipment obligations, all of which were successfully resolved. The entire project took 13 months from initial discussions until contract closing.

Worldwide Sales & Marketing

Question: Please elaborate on your experience in worldwide sales and marketing within the consumer products industry. The combination of your sales, marketing, key account, and global experience is what prompted us to call you in for an interview.

Your Response: Building top-producing global markets is what I do best. No matter the country, the language barriers, or the government red tape, I have consistently produced well beyond expectations and delivered double-digit revenue growth within each market. Here are some notable results from the past three years: In 2001, I launched a new consumer product into the Latin American market that outperformed projections by 80% and generated more than $22 million in new sales revenues. In 2002, I transferred to the Far Eastern market, launched another new product and closed over $45 million in sales-225% over projections. Then, in 2003, I assumed full sales responsibility for all product lines throughout Germany, Switzerland, and the Netherlands. We closed the year at 135% of quota with a $90 million revenue stream; now the region is poised for even stronger growth in 2004.

KeyWord Accomplishment Phrases for Interviews, Resumes, & Cover Letters

Cross-Border Transactions

- Personally structured and negotiated $5.5 million in cross-border transactions among various Latin American countries to facilitate market growth, expansion, and diversification.

Cross-Cultural Business Relations

- Appointed General Manager of Technology Commercialization for IBM based largely on demonstrated expertise in cross-cultural business relations, communications, and negotiations with foreign dignitaries throughout the Pacific Rim.

Foreign Government Relations

- Managed foreign government relations with top officials throughout Nepal during the construction and commissioning of the country's first hydroelectric power plant, a $40 million infrastructure development project.

Global Business Development

- Defined Bayer's global business development strategy, which resulted in its successful and profitable expansion into the Australian market, now a $2.2 billion dollar revenue generator for the company.

Import & Export Operations

- Streamlined Maersk's Import and Export Division with the introduction of simplified work processes, new technologies, and a more talented and committed workforce. Resulted in a 20% reduction in operating costs and 28% improvement in net profitability.

International Trade

- Structured and funded sophisticated international trade transactions for Smith Barney's International Division. Over the past three years, closed over $5 billion in deals between the U.S. and countries throughout the Southern African continent.

Joint Ventures

- Identified emerging opportunities and structured three joint ventures between Macy's and Harrod's as part of their cooperative effort to expand into India and Pakistan, a region with market potential identified in the hundreds of millions of dollars.

Mergers & Acquisitions

- Retained by one of the most successful venture capital firms in the history of the U.S. to structure and negotiate all of their merger and acquisition activity within the natural resources industry. To date, have closed six mergers and two acquisitions with total investment of more than $4.9 million.

Multinational Contract Negotiations

- Directed a team of attorneys, accountants, financial analysts, and sales executives handling Amoco's multinational contract negotiations, contract amendments, and contract close-outs for development projects worldwide. Individual contracts were valued from $250,000 to over $1 billion.

Worldwide Sales & Marketing

- Led a 45-person worldwide sales and marketing organization that closed 2002 at 275% of budget, 2003 at 160% of budget, and is projected to close 2004 at 205% of budget.

Your Personal KeyWord Toolkit

Use the space below to add in KeyWords and KeyWord Phrases from your own career in International Business. Once you've done that, you'll want to do three more things essential to the success of your job search campaign.

1. Write KeyWord accomplishment phrases for each new KeyWord and KeyWord Phrase on your list. Then, use those words in your resume, cover letters, and interviews.

2. Write KeyWord interview responses to use when each of those KeyWord topics comes up. That way, you'll be instantly prepared with answers that effectively highlight your accomplishments, key projects, record of promotion, honors and awards, and other distinguishing aspects of your career.

3. Practice #1 and #2 above over and over! Although it certainly isn't necessary that you memorize each and every accomplishment and interview response, it is essential that the moment the topic comes up during an interview, you're immediately prepared to answer.

Your KeyWords & KeyWord Phrases:

_____

_____

_____

_____

_____

_____

_____

_____

_____

_____

Chapter 14

KeyWords for the Legal Professional

Top 10 KeyWords & KeyWord Phrases

Briefs, Pleadings, Motions, & Memoranda
Client Representation
Defense
Discovery & Investigation
Judicial Proceedings
Law Enforcement
Legal Advocacy
Litigation
Prosecution
VIP Protection

KeyWord Interview Q&A

Briefs, Pleadings, Motions, & Memoranda

Question: First of all, congratulations on passing the bar exam on your first attempt. It is an achievement that you should be quite proud of and one that really does impress us. So, now that you're looking for your first associate-level position, can you please summarize your experience in drafting briefs, pleadings, motions, and memoranda?

Your Response: As a legal intern with the Commodity Futures Trading Commission, I supported the efforts of a team of attorneys working on a diversity of Freedom of Information Act cases. Specifically, I wrote briefs, pleadings, motions, and memoranda, some of which supported the release of information under the Act; others that did not. In addition, I revised annotations on Administrative Rules of Practice and coordinated the implementation of a new technology system to automate the brief-writing process. For the latter project, I was awarded an exemplary service commendation as it has reduced the number of man-hours required for drafting briefs by better than 35%.

Client Representation

Question: Providing comprehensive client representation for the more than 500 corporations we serve is of vital importance to the continued success of our firm. In what particular disciplines have you represented clients?

Your Response: I've been quite fortunate in my career with Holden, Boldsworth and Stark. Over the past nine years, I've represented clients in virtually all areas of business law including, but not limited to, corporate, real estate, taxation, antitrust, copyright, employment, workers compensation, environmental, intellectual property, SEC affairs, international, and unfair competition. What's most important, I have won more than 80% of the cases I have managed, whether won in a courtroom, at mediation, or at arbitration.

Defense

Question: What has been the most prominent criminal defense case in which you've been involved? And was this case successfully defended?

Your Response: Undoubtedly, my most prominent criminal defense case involved representing one of our corporate clients indicted by the FBI on 182 counts of mail and wire fraud. The case received extensive press coverage as a result of this individual's prominent standing within the business community, so each and every legal action we took was widely reported and dissected by the media and their legal experts. My challenge, despite the high visibility of this case, was to defend this individual from alleged illegal actions as well as the increasingly negative community response. Through thorough investigation and review of thousands of pages of documentation, my defense team and I were able to clearly document that this individual had not committed any felony and was indeed innocent. The trial lasted 59 days and involved hundreds of witnesses on behalf of both the prosecution and defense. Because our legal strategy and evidence were solid, our client was acquitted of all wrongdoing.

Discovery & Investigation

Question: Many attorneys feel that unless they're in the courtroom, they're not really practicing law to the full extent for which they've been trained. However, as we all know, the behind-the-scenes work of discovery and investigation is really the foundation for any successful legal defense or prosecution. As such, what has been your experience in discovery and investigation?

Your Response: Fortunately, I am not one of the attorneys who believes that in order to truly practice law that I must stand up in the courtroom. To the contrary, I find the tasks of discovery and investigation to be those most critical to any case. Without the necessary intelligence, I cannot defend or prosecute anyone alleged to have committed an illegal act. In my first four years out of law school, I devoted 100% of my time to discovery and investigation. Now, as a Senior Attorney with my firm, I oversee the team responsible for these functions for all the cases I handle for alleged incidents of racketeering, fraud, and other white-collar crimes.

Judicial Proceedings

Question: How much time have you spent in the courtroom and how familiar are you with judicial proceedings and actions?

Your Response: Currently, I spend an average of 60% of my time in both state and federal courtrooms. As such, I have a wealth of experience in how the judicial system operates, specific judicial proceedings and their ramifications, and both routine and non-routine judicial actions. In fact, based on my experience, I was selected several years ago to manage the courtroom indoctrination and training program for all new attorneys hired into our firm. I find this to be a particularly rewarding assignment where I can mentor and develop the individuals who will, at some point, become our senior legal staff. Understanding the interconnections between the legal and judicial disciplines is one of the most critical efforts in developing lawyers who can function well in both environments and provide their clients with the best legal representation possible.

Law Enforcement

Question: Our goal in bringing in a new Chief of Police is to recruit an individual who is committed to strengthening our law enforcement practices and reducing our ever-increasing crime rate. As the Chief of Police in Erie County, what have you done to improve law enforcement practices and reduce your crime rate?

Your Response: My career with Erie County is one that I'm quite proud of. Under my leadership, we have reduced non-violent crimes 28% and violent crimes 35% over the past five years. This has been accomplished through a variety of efforts; most significantly, by better training and leadership of our officers, and by encouraging the community to be more proactive in alerting the authorities to alleged criminal activity. By encouraging cooperation between the police department and the community, we've changed our law enforcement environment to one that is proactive, not reactive, and responsive to the needs of our citizens.

Legal Advocacy

Question: In reviewing your resume, you briefly mentioned your work in legal advocacy on behalf of the state of Minnesota's Child Protective Services Division. I know that this was several years ago, but can you please elaborate on your experience? This is of particular interest to our agency.

Your Response: Working as a legal advocate on behalf of abused and abandoned children has been the greatest contribution of my career. I must admit that I fell into the position as a result of a recommendation from a past colleague, and although I had no previous experience representing children, I found the work to be extremely fulfilling. All of these children were in need of strong legal representation and advocacy in the most difficult of situations and with repercussions that the children often did not understand. However, I succeeded time and time again in taking these children from their homes and placing them in safe and nurturing environments where they could thrive. After that experience and the tremendous impact it left, I have devoted my career to legal advocacy on behalf of not only children but adults in need of legal protection and advocacy.

Litigation

Question: We're most interested in bringing an Attorney into our practice who has a wealth of experience in tax litigation. Would you consider this to be an area of your expertise?

Your Response: As a corporate litigator with Marsh and McClelland, I have been particularly active in defending our corporate clients against alleged tax violations at both the state and federal level. I consider myself extremely effective in developing tax litigation strategies, and have a unique expertise in the critical analysis of tax implications relative to international business transactions such as mergers, acquisitions, joint ventures, and other corporate development projects. In addition, I have a wealth of experience in litigating state, corporate, partnership, and income tax issues, and have successfully represented more than 50 U.S. corporations in these proceedings.

Prosecution

Question: What is your track of success as a Prosecutor with the DA's office in Sonoma County?

Your Response: Over the past five years, I've prosecuted a total of 150 drug trafficking cases with 148 convictions and only two acquittals. This is one of the highest prosecution rates in the history of Sonoma County and a record of which I am particularly proud. I joined the DA's office solely to investigate and prosecute drug offenders and, as evidenced, have been extremely effective in this effort.

VIP Protection

Question: With the ever-increasing threat of terrorism, we've determined that we must increase our VIP protection to ensure the safety of our executive staff, particularly those who travel internationally. Do you have any experience in VIP protection services?

Your Response: One of my primary responsibilities as Director of Security Operations for Chase Manhattan is the management of the company's VIP protection programs both domestically and internationally. This includes the recruitment and training of all security personnel, emergency response planning and preparedness, incident response and investigation, travel and long-term security planning. Obviously, a great deal of what I manage in this regard is confidential; however, I can share with you the fact that last year we were able to halt a potential terrorist attack on one of our principals through my team's expertise in collecting and analyzing incoming intelligence information. We immediately heightened our VIP protection 24/7, consulted with state and federal law enforcement officials, and provided the information necessary for a major arrest.

KeyWord Accomplishment Phrases for Interviews, Resumes, and Cover Letters

Briefs, Pleadings, Motions, & Memoranda

- Completed a six-month internship writing briefs, pleadings, motions, and memoranda on behalf of four assistant DAs in the Fraud Investigation Division.

Client Representation

- Provided pro-bono representation for indigent clients arrested for drug misdemeanor charges in a direct effort to reduce the escalating costs associated with non-felony arrests.

Defense

- Appointed to the three-attorney defense team representing Enron executives in civil court proceedings pertaining to the disposition of assets and satisfaction of multi-million-dollar liabilities due to the Internal Revenue Service and state tax agencies.

Discovery & Investigation

- Hired from a pool of more than 25 competitive candidates to join the prestigious law firm of McCormick & Dowdy as a member of its corporate discovery and investigation team.

Judicial Proceedings

- Authored university textbook on the most recent changes in judicial proceedings and their direct impact on legal representation of white-collar and blue-collar criminal activities.

Law Enforcement

- Restructured and restaffed local law enforcement agencies throughout Texas to more effectively handle the ever-increasing incidence of illegal immigration from Mexico. Efforts resulted in a 22% reduction in the number of illegal aliens crossing into Texas from points along the Rio Grande.

Legal Advocacy

- Appointed the state's legal advocate for non-English-speaking adults seeking political asylum in the U.S. Personally managed a caseload of more than 500 persons in 2003.

Litigation

- Expert litigator with a track record of more than 200 wins in both state and federal court proceedings.

Prosecution

- Member of the state's prosecution team that successfully prosecuted more than 20 members of the Cardoza Family in Colombia, a joint U.S.-Colombia effort to shut down a major flow of cocaine into North America.

VIP Protection

- Hired by the Board of Directors of Mercantile Bank & Trust to provide 24/7 VIP protection services to all Board members and corporate executives following intelligence warning of potential incidents by a disgruntled employee.

Your Personal KeyWord Toolkit

Use the space on the next page to add in KeyWords and KeyWord Phrases from your own career as a Legal professional. Once you've done that, you'll want to do three more things essential to the success of your job search campaign.

1. Write KeyWord accomplishment phrases for each new KeyWord and KeyWord Phrase on your list. Then, use those words in your resume, cover letters, and interviews.

2. Write KeyWord interview responses to use when each of those KeyWord topics comes up. That way, you'll be instantly prepared with answers that effectively highlight your accomplishments, key projects, record of promotion, honors and awards, and other distinguishing aspects of your career.

3. Practice #1 and #2 above over and over! Although it certainly isn't necessary that you memorize each and every accomplishment and interview response, it is essential that the moment the topic comes up during an interview, you're immediately prepared to answer.

Your KeyWords & KeyWord Phrases:

_____

_____

_____

_____

_____

_____

_____

_____

_____

_____

Chapter 15

KeyWords for the Manufacturing Professional

Top 10 KeyWords & KeyWord Phrases

Capital Projects
Facilities Management & Expansion
Logistics
Operations Management
Process Automation
Product Manufacturability
Productivity Improvement
Quality Assurance
Warehousing & Distribution
Workforce Management

KeyWord Interview Q&A

Capital Projects

Question: Our ideal candidate for this position will have substantial experience in the planning, budgeting, and management of capital projects ranging dramatically in their composition. What has been your specific involvement in this area and why are you interested in our position?

Your Response: Throughout my eight-year tenure with Nokia, I have participated in and/or led more than 20 capital improvement projects. This has included facilities expansions, technology installations, equipment retrofits, infrastructure development, and several production area redesign projects. Total investment in these projects was approximately $12 million. I'm interested in your position for the same reason that I've so enjoyed these projects…I thrive on diversity. When managing projects of this magnitude, it is essential that one be successful in managing a wide range of project personnel and resources, some from within the company and many from outside. Coordinating all of these different components of each project is where I have excelled. I am a skilled planner, scheduler, problem solver, and consensus builder, each of which are critical tasks to ensure the smooth, cost-effective, and timely completion of all of our projects.

Facilities Management & Expansion

Question: Funding has been approved and we are just beginning to set up the facilities management team that will direct a $4.2 million expansion project. What are the largest facilities management projects that you've ever managed?

Your Response: As the Director of Facilities Management for Armstrong's largest production plant, I am directly responsible for a 35-acre, 12-building complex. In this capacity, I manage daily facilities operations, all industrial and plant engineering projects, new construction and renovations, major technology and building systems installations, and scores of retrofit projects. Most notably, we just completed a $2.8 million new construction project that was directly under my leadership. The new building, an R&D facility, was projected to cost more than $3.2 million. Working in cooperation with the engineering team, I redesigned several key areas within the building, replaced costly vendors with others supplying equal equipment at a lower cost, and rescheduled the entire building cycle. As such, we captured cost savings of $400,000 and delivered the project two months ahead of schedule.

Logistics

Question: Our logistics manager is the individual responsible for the entire warehousing, distribution, fleet management, and delivery operation for the midwestern United States. Why do you believe you're qualified to manage such a huge operation?

Your Response: I will guarantee you that I can successfully direct your operation because I have managed quite similar operations for one of your major competitors. In fact, the only reason I'm leaving the company is that they've decided to transition their logistics operations to a third-party provider who has assured them that they can reduce costs. I'm not so sure, but that's a whole different story. Under my leadership, our integrated logistics operations, which include 16 warehouses, a 180-vehicle fleet, a staff of 92, and distribution to more than 500 locations throughout the eastern U.S., has performed extremely well and within tight budget constraints. In fact, we reduced our operating costs by 12% last year while increasing the volume of products that we move by 8%. Our customer satisfaction rating is at an all-time high of 92% and we've had no customer attrition in the past two years. This is just a sampling of what I can do for you.

Operations Management

Question: As the Operations Manager with Delco, what has been your most significant achievement?

Your Response: Without a doubt, my most significant contribution to the company has been my ability to effectively handle such a wide range of operating management functions. In fact, now that the company knows I am leaving my position to relocate to Austin, they've decided to hire two new employees to handle everything that I currently manage alone. To summarize, I direct production planning and scheduling, operating and capital budgets, materials flow, quality, manufacturing engineering, machine shop operations, staffing, training, safety, and the entire logistics function. Fortunately, I have a team of eight supervisors, each of whom is responsible for one key operating function. Together, we have successfully managed the operation for the past four years, met or exceeded all of our production and cost objectives, and created a model operating division that has served as the benchmark for all new operations the company is setting up throughout North America.

Process Automation

Question: What has been your specific experience in process automation and simplification?

Your Response: I'm sure that what attracted you to my background is the combination of my experience in engineering, manufacturing, and technology. As an engineer, I am constantly striving to improve our product designs. As a manufacturer, I work to improve product manufacturability and production yields. As a technologist, I am able to create and use the right tools to ensure that both the engineering and manufacturing functions operate at their optimum levels. To achieve that, many of my contributions to Kohler have been in the development and implementation of process automation tools for a diversity of functions, from machining and prototyping to actual floor manufacturing, materials movement, quality assurance, and industrial engineering functions. Although many of these automation and simplification functions cannot be individually measured to determine their impact on the total operation, I can tell you that my efforts have contributed to double-digit gains in production yields and double-digit reductions in annual operating and overhead costs.

Product Manufacturability

Question: Improving the transition of products from design engineering to the production floor is one of our greatest challenges and one of our most critical operating goals. Often the cycle is considerably longer than our initial projections. Can you relate any experience you have in this particular function?

Your Response: One of the functions that allows IBM to perform so effectively in managing its product development pipeline is the fact that a minimum of three manufacturing personnel are assigned to each and every product development team. And, in fact, this has been one of the most rewarding functions of my job. Working in cooperation with a team of design engineers, I have provided manufacturing guidance and leadership for the development of more than 20 new products, product line extensions, and accessories that now generate combined annual revenues well in excess of $100 million. By closely monitoring all design activities and immediately implementing corrective actions to enhance product manufacturability, I have saved the company millions of dollars in potential wasted time and effort. This has been one of several reasons why I've been so quickly promoted and to such a high level of responsibility at such a young age.

Productivity Improvement

Question: We need a producer in this position…an individual who can quickly gain control of our manufacturing floor, identify areas of inefficiency, and deliver measurable gains in production yields. Have you been successful in increasing productivity in your previous assignments?

Your Response: Yes, in each of my positions, my teams and I have improved productivity and the efficiency of operations. In my current production management position, productivity has increased 26% over the past two years. This was accomplished primarily by increasing materials availability on the floor and redesigning staffing patterns to more accurately reflect production demand. Previously, with Merck, I was able to improve production yields 18% in just one year by eliminating obvious bottlenecks in production flow. And, finally, as a first-line manufacturing floor supervisor with Pfizer, production yield in my area increased 31%, a huge jump again attributed to better materials management and improved equipment maintenance. As my track record demonstrates, I deliver results and will continue to do so for you.

Quality Assurance

Question: Improving the quality assurance function in our organization is one of our primary goals over the next two years. As a QA Manager for Motorola, what have you done to improve quality performance and how?

Your Response: I'm delighted to hear that you're so committed to improving your quality function, for I believe it is one of the most vital functions within any manufacturing organization. Unfortunately, all too many companies get lost in the quality documentation process and don't fully understand how to translate the data into action. That certainly has not been the case within my QA organization. Over the past three years, not only have I orchestrated a complete revitalization of our quality function, I have also prepared the operation for ISO 9000 and ISO 14001 certifications, both of which we have received. What's more, I have reduced quality defects in finished products by 18% which roughly translates to a $2 million net annual savings. Our QA programs have been so successful that they now serve as the model for the entire Motorola organization worldwide.

Warehousing & Distribution

Question: Please detail the most complex warehousing and distribution system you've ever managed and how well you managed it.

Your Response: Although I am responsible for warehousing, distribution, materials, and logistics in my current position, the assignment that most accurately reflects the depth of my experience was as a Warehouse Manager for Ryder Dedicated Logistics. In that position, I managed three warehouses in the Seattle area distributing products to 15 different retail clients throughout Washington, Oregon, California, Idaho, and Nevada. These were 24/7 operations receiving products from more than 100 suppliers. All products were documented upon receipt, stored in the appropriate areas of each warehouse, and then loaded and shipped to each customer destination. In total, we handled over two million tons of product annually. Most representative of my success in this position was the fact that we achieved and maintained a better than 95% on-time distribution to all 15 customers.

Workforce Management

Question: One of the most challenging functions of the position of production supervisor is managing our diverse workforce of more than 500 hourly personnel. Have you ever managed a workforce this large?

Your Response: Training and supervising hourly personnel can indeed be a challenging assignment and one in which I have excelled. Currently, I direct a staff of 250. In my previous position, I supervised a staff of 100 plus. In both positions, I've been successful in increasing worker productivity and reducing employee absenteeism by implementing appropriate training and incentive programs designed specifically for an hourly workforce. In fact, in my current position, productivity has improved 22%, efficiency 18%, and the quality of finished products by 12%, the first increases the company has experienced in over five years.

KeyWord Accomplishment Phrases for Interviews, Resumes, & Cover Letters

Capital Projects

- Planned, staffed, budgeted, and directed over $20 million in capital improvement and expansion projects over the past year. Delivered one project at $250,000 under budget, another two months ahead of schedule, and all others within budget and on schedule.

Facilities Management & Expansion

- Managed a 22-acre poultry production facility, $2.8 million in facility expansion projects, and a $12 million annual facilities operating budget. Slashed facility costs by $1.2 million by restructuring staff scheduling and implementing technology tools.

Logistics

- Appointed as the first-ever Logistics Manager responsible for integrating all purchasing, distribution, warehousing, and logistics function into one organization as part of Saturn's push to reduce costs, improve operations, and outpace emerging competition.

Operations Management

- As Operations Manager, implemented SAP technology, ISO 9001 standards, and product reliability measures that immediately improved productivity 15% on all electronic components and replacement parts.

Process Automation

- Tasked with introducing a quality-based process automation program for all machine-shop operations, resulting in an 18% gain in production efficiency, 15% reduction in manual documentation requirements, and 100% increase in employee satisfaction.

Product Manufacturability

- Liaison between Engineering and Manufacturing Departments to ensure ease in manufacturability as more than 20 new products moved from R&D pipeline into full-scale production. New products generated $1.1 million in revenues within first year.

Productivity Improvement

- Introduced lean manufacturing techniques and manufacturing cells into DynCorp's operations. Improved productivity 24%, reduced scrap 42%, and increased product reliability 48%.

Quality Assurance

- Planned and led implementation of a series of quality assurance and quality improvement initiatives including successful ISO 9000 and ISO 14000 audits, positioning Merck as the pharmaceutical industry's forerunner in quality performance.

Warehousing & Distribution

- Spearheaded Airborne's transition to an entirely automated warehousing and distribution function utilizing the most recent GPS technology commercially available. Projections forecast a 20% reduction in routing costs, 10% reduction in delivery times, and measurable improvement in customer satisfaction.

Workforce Management

- Implemented a series of workforce management initiatives including pay-for-performance incentives, attendance incentives, an employee recognition program, and a monthly employee-management meeting to discuss and resolve manufacturing floor issues impacting productivity.

Your Personal KeyWord Toolkit

Use the space on the next page to add in KeyWords and KeyWord Phrases from your own career in Manufacturing. Once you've done that, you'll want to do three more things essential to the success of your job search campaign.

1. Write KeyWord accomplishment phrases for each new KeyWord and KeyWord Phrase on your list. Then, use those words in your resume, cover letters, and interviews.

2. Write KeyWord interview responses to use when each of those KeyWord topics comes up. That way, you'll be instantly prepared with answers that effectively highlight your accomplishments, key projects, record of promotion, honors and awards, and other distinguishing aspects of your career.

3. Practice #1 and #2 above over and over! Although it certainly isn't necessary that you memorize each and every accomplishment and interview response,

it is essential that the moment the topic comes up during an interview, you're immediately prepared to answer.

Your KeyWords & KeyWord Phrases:

_____

_____

_____

_____

_____

_____

_____

_____

_____

_____

Chapter 16

KeyWords for the Retail Professional

Top 10 KeyWords & KeyWord Phrases

Buying
Customer Loyalty
Customer Service
Department Management
Inventory Planning & Control
Loss Prevention
Merchandising
Product Planning & Positioning
Retail Store Operations
Sales & Sales Management

KeyWord Interview Q&A

Buying

Question: Now that we're expanding into consumer hardware product lines, we're most interested in a candidate with specific buying experience within that market. Can you please highlight any related experience you offer.

Your Response: As a Buyer with Home Depot for the past five years, I've been directly responsible for the entire buying function for more than 200 different consumer hardware product lines. In summary, I am responsible for vendor sourcing and selection, pricing, contract negotiations, buying, and product delivery. Most significantly, I have identified scores of new suppliers that never serviced Home Depot in the past. Through my negotiations with them, I've accomplished two notable things. First, I've reduced the annual purchasing costs for my assigned product lines by an average of 8%. Second, by selecting the right suppliers, I've increased the on-time receipt of our orders by better than 20%, thus ensuring we have adequate inventory on hand to meet consumer demand.

Customer Loyalty

Question: In today's intensely competitive retail marketplace, it is essential that we be able to increase our customer loyalty and retention to ensure that we meet our aggressive revenue and profit goals. Do you have any direct experience in developing customer loyalty programs and, if so, what were the results?

Your Response: One of the primary reasons for my rapid promotion with Macy's has been my success in creating retail operations that promote customer loyalty. I've achieved this through the design and implementation of numerous customer programs that acknowledged their business, rewarded their loyalty, and encouraged their continued business with special rebates and other incentives. When I arrived at Macy's in Newark, customer retention was 72%. Today, five years later, under my leadership, our retention numbers average 90% to 92%, an exceptional achievement within the competitive retail industry.

Customer Service

Question: Our Customer Service Department is one of the busiest in the store, so we need someone with the ability to work well under pressure. How have you handled yourself previously in such fast-paced, high-volume operations?

Your Response: I can remember two years ago, right after Christmas, when in just one day, we handled over 800 customers. They were 40 deep in line and I'd never seen anything like it before. If there was ever a time in my life that I displayed calm within the storm, it was that day. Never letting the smile leave my face, and remaining friendly despite the behavior of certain customers, I still look back on that day with confidence. I now know that I can manage anything that any customer service department can throw my way!

Department Management

Question: As the Manager of the Men's Clothing Department for the Hecht Company, please describe your overall areas of responsibility.

Your Response: Bottom line, I'm responsible for the successful financial performance of the department. Over the past two years, I have increased department revenues by an average of 28% annually, reduced our staffing costs 11%, and improved overall profitability 24%. And, for my success, I've been awarded seven "Department Manager of the Month" awards! In terms of day-to-day responsibilities, they include staffing, training, and scheduling of all full- and part-time personnel, sales and customer service, departmental budgeting, daily and monthly sales and expense reporting, merchandising, promotions, and all inventory management functions. In addition, I consult on a routine basis with the retail buying staff regarding merchandise selection, with the advertising staff for weekly product sales, and with the Store Manager to coordinate long-term business planning.

Inventory Planning & Control

Question: We're looking for a candidate who not only has a great deal of experience in purchasing, but a candidate with a solid background in inventory planning and control. Can you address your experience in this area?

Your Response: As a Buyer, the scope of my responsibility includes the entire supply chain function. Specifically, I manage purchasing, vendor selection, all related budgeting and financial reporting affairs, and the entire inventory planning function. In addition, I supervise a staff of 12. I particularly enjoy the inventory management activities because of their diversity. One minute I'm working with a store manager to project product requirements; the next, I'm coordinating schedules for inventory movement throughout our store and six others within the region. Where I've excelled is in reducing inventory carrying costs by implementing a JIT system where, believe it or not, one never existed. As a result, carrying costs have been reduced by 35%.

Loss Prevention

Question: I'm most interested in bringing in a Store Operations Manager with substantial experience and success in reducing store losses and implementing loss prevention programs. What have you accomplished in this area?

Your Response: When I arrived at McClelland's, annual store losses from both internal and external theft were in the tens of thousands of dollars. In fact, the Store Manager was relatively certain that employee theft alone had jumped more than 20% over the past year. My challenge was to halt those losses immediately and I did it. Within two months, losses had dropped by more than 50%; two months later, an additional 22%. I accomplished this through the use of both technological and human resources, implementing the necessary merchandise control and facilities monitoring equipment that was lacking, and introducing a no-tolerance program for employee theft.

Merchandising

Question: What do you believe makes you more qualified than other candidates who are interested in joining our merchandising team?

Your Response: The unique combination of my retail sales experience, along with my degree in visual design and graphic arts, places me in a uniquely qualified position to be a Merchandiser. Not only do I understand the retail industry and how customers select their products, I also have an excellent eye for aesthetic design and product placement. I love to create displays where the display and the merchandise become one; I enjoy working with lighting, color, textiles, and design; I strive to create an environment that encourages people to touch and feel, and we all know that act alone is a huge step toward actual purchase. I guarantee that the combination of my skills will be truly valuable to your merchandising team.

Product Planning & Positioning

Question: Determining what products to purchase for our stores and how to best position them is one of the greatest challenges any retailer faces. Please describe your overall experience as it relates to this particular function.

Your Response: I believe that product planning and positioning is all about forecasting and being one step ahead of the competition. We have to know what our customers will want in six months and begin to market those products long before our competitors have even considered introducing them. If a retailer can do this, he will succeed and establish a clear and distinct market position. One of my greatest successes was the introduction of Brighton products into our store before anyone had ever heard of Brighton. That product line alone now generates millions of dollars in annual revenues and clearly defines our upscale market position.

Retail Store Operations

Question: As a Retail Store Operations Manager for Lowe's, please describe your specific areas of responsibility.

Your Response: In my current position, I am responsible for a staff of 12, all facilities management and improvement projects, loss prevention, merchandise handling, and inventory control and movement. In addition, the Store Sales Manager, Customer Service Manager, and I work closely in the areas of staffing, employee training, and cost control. And, together, we've been a great team. Store sales increased 16% last year, we reduced costs 8%, and improved our profitability 11%.

Sales & Sales Management

Question: We looking for two things in a candidate. One, we want a sales producer, someone who has a strong track record of sales experience. Second, we want a sales manager, someone who has trained and led retail sales teams that have also performed well. Are you that candidate?

Your Response: Without a doubt, I am your candidate as I'm the perfect balance between sales producer and sales manager. I began my retail career as a Sales Associate and was promoted quickly through a series of increasingly responsible sales positions based largely on my ability to sell. In fact, I was the top producer for four years running while at Dillard's. Now, although sales is only one component of my job, I am still consistently ranked as one of the top 10 sales producers throughout the entire Southwestern market. As a Sales Manager, I've been equally successful in recruiting and training other top producers and implementing a culture of quality-based sales and customer service. As a result, sales under my leadership have increased between 18% and 26% each year for the past six years.

KeyWord Accomplishment Phrases for Interviews, Resumes, & Cover Letters

Buying

- As a Senior Buyer with Macy's, purchased over $500 million annually in women's and children's clothing from major designers in New York, London, Paris, and Madrid. Retail sales value of merchandise exceeded $500 million annually.

Customer Loyalty

- Introduced a customer loyalty program that increased repeat clientele to more than 70% of the entire customer base, solidifying Hecht's position as the #1 retailer in the Mid-Atlantic states.

Customer Service

- Designed and taught customer service training programs to more than 1,000 sales and support employees of Target, resulting in a 22% increase in customer satisfaction ratings when all other regional competitors were losing customer base due to poor service and quality issues.

Department Management

- Promoted from Senior Sales Associate to Department Manager with full buying, merchandising, sales, staffing, training, and customer service responsibility for the company's $2 million Housewares Department. Delivered a minimum 10% increase in net profits for four consecutive years.

Inventory Planning & Control

- Automated the previously manual inventory planning and control function, which reduced number of required employees by 50% while effectively handling annual growth of more than 20% in product volume and sales.

Loss Prevention

- Implemented multi-unit loss prevention program that reduced employee and customer store theft by more than 25%, equivalent to more than $500,000 in annual merchandise losses.

Merchandising

- Won the 2002 "Merchandiser of the Year" award, out of 125 merchandisers, for demonstrated expertise in product selection, merchandising, and promotion.

Product Planning & Positioning

- Spearheaded corporate task force challenged to redefine the company's product planning and positioning strategy to keep pace with encroaching competition from other moderately priced retailers entering the marketplace.

Retail Store Operations

- In a downward spiraling economy, successfully increased sales revenues an average of 12% per retail store through a company-wide commitment to product quality and customer service.

Sales & Sales Management

- Advanced from sales position to sales management assignment with full P&L responsibility for the operations of a $2.8 million Lowe's in central Virginia. Delivered 12% profit improvement in 2001, 15% in 2002, and 22% in 2003.

Your Personal KeyWord Toolkit

Use the space on the next page to add in KeyWords and KeyWord Phrases from your own career in Retail. Once you've done that, you'll want to do three more things essential to the success of your job search campaign.

1. Write KeyWord accomplishment phrases for each new KeyWord and KeyWord Phrase on your list. Then, use those words in your resume, cover letters, and interviews.

2. Write KeyWord interview responses to use when each of those KeyWord topics comes up. That way, you'll be instantly prepared with answers that effectively highlight your accomplishments, key projects, record of promotion, honors and awards, and other distinguishing aspects of your career.

3. Practice #1 and #2 above over and over! Although it certainly isn't necessary that you memorize each and every accomplishment and interview response, it is essential that the moment the topic comes up during an interview, you're immediately prepared to answer.

Your KeyWords and KeyWord Phrases:

_____

_____

_____

_____

_____

_____

_____

_____

Chapter 17

KeyWords for the
Sales & Marketing Professional

Top 10 KeyWords & KeyWord Phrases

Account Management & Retention
Competitive Wins
Customer Relationship Management
Multi-Channel Distribution
New Business Development
New Product Launch
Sales Negotiations
Sales Training & Team Leadership
Strategic Marketing
Territory Management

KeyWord Interviewing Q&A

Account Management & Retention

Question: One of our greatest challenges is the management and retention of our account relationships as the volume of our competitors has increased. Can you elaborate on your experience in this area?

Your Response: My entire account management philosophy centers around the fact that in order to succeed, I must own the customer relationship. Specifically, I must position myself and the companies and products that I represent as sole-source providers to my accounts for any products that they need which fall within my portfolio. By utilizing this approach, I have been extremely successful in the field. In my current position, I manage relationships with more than 100 wholesale accounts within the agricultural industry. Over the past year, I've retained 98% of my customers; the 2% who left went out of business. In my previous sales position with Heinhold Farms, I retained an average of 92% of my accounts for five consecutive years, despite increasing competition with lower pricing. My customers knew that I would deliver and that I would provide the individualized service they were accustomed to receiving.

Competitive Wins

Question: Being able to sell and win against the competition is our most desirable qualification for each sales associate that we hire. Can you provide one or two examples of your success in competitive sales?

Your Response: Just this past month, I closed a $25,000 sale with Coleman-Adams Construction. This was an intensely competitive sales contract where I was one of more than 20 equipment manufacturers attempting to close the deal. I won the contract based on my previous history of sales and service to the company, despite the fact that I was not the lowest bidder. I learned early in my career that winning against the competition is based on three critical factors - my rapport with the decision-makers, the performance and reliability of my products, and my commitment to quality customer service.

Customer Relationship Management

Question: The primary responsibility of the position we are currently hiring for is the management of our customer relationships. What is your personal customer management philosophy?

Your Response: My philosophy is that to consistently win I must own the customer relationship. Specifically, my goal is to capture a new account and then position my company as the preferred provider, able to meet any and all customer needs as they relate to accounting and auditing services. I want my customers to know that no matter what they need, I can either provide the service, make the appropriate referral, or research and identify the appropriate service or information. There should never be any other accounting firm they need; I am their sole provider and will continue to manage that relationship for as long as we are working cooperatively. It's all about building relationships and working them to the utmost satisfaction of the customer.

Multi-Channel Distribution

Question: We're just beginning to expand our distribution through a variety of channels and not rely entirely on a direct sales force. Have you ever established a third-party distribution network?

Your Response: In my current position with Merck, as well as my previous position with Pfizer, I managed both direct and indirect sales forces. For Merck, I expanded their third-party distribution to include a network of independent manufacturers' representatives. Within one year of establishing this network, we were able to increase the sale of our pharmaceutical products by 23%, which is equivalent to roughly $18 million in new revenues. With Pfizer, I realigned their distribution network, integrated it more closely with the direct sales force, and delivered over $200 million in sales within a three-year period. All of this was accomplished by selecting the right distributors, training them in our products, and providing strategic guidance in negotiating and closing key account relationships.

New Business Development

Question: The current thrust of our sales and marketing organization is on new business development. Have you participated and/or led any major new product development initiatives?

Your Response: Developing new business and building new account relationships is what I do best. In my current position with RX Technology, I was hired with precisely that mission - to build new business with major retailers nationwide for the introduction of our next-generation POS technology. Starting with virtually nothing, I created an entire marketing strategy and campaign, directed creative design and writing teams responsible for all sales collaterals, and personally called on top executives of more than 200 prospective accounts. Within year one, I had closed better than 80% of those accounts for a new annual revenue stream of more than $250 million.

New Product Launch

Question: We're most interested in a candidate with an extensive background in launching new products. Can you address your level of experience in this area?

Your Response: New product launch has been the hallmark of my career. In total, I've been responsible for and/or participated in the launch of more than 20 new products for Johnson & Johnson over the past five years, and believe the total annual revenues from these new products now generate more than $200 million. One of my most recent projects was the introduction of a new designer hand-cream product line where my involvement began in the early stages of product development. I was appointed Chief Marketing Officer for this initiative, working directly with product design and manufacturing teams to create a product in direct response to customer demand. We fast-tracked the project, bringing it from initial design to market launch in just under 14 months. To date, these products have generated more than $30 million in U.S. sales in just 36 months. Now, I'm taking the project one step further and assembling all the resources for a global market launch in early 2005.

Sales Negotiations

Question: The individual leaving our current position as Sales Manager for the Detroit market has performed exceptionally well in highly competitive sales negotiations. As such, it is vital that we replace her with another equally talented negotiator. Can you detail your most competitive contract negotiation and how you won?

Your Response: Last year we were faced with a critical situation. Our largest account was considering switching to another paper supplier, which would have had an extremely negative impact on our market position. I was chosen by the President of the company to personally handle sales negotiations and retain the account. Over the next two months, I negotiated with top personnel throughout the organization - the President and CEO, the COO, the office manager, and several production managers. In each and every communication, I stressed the importance of their account to our company, our commitment to them and their continued satisfaction, and our ability to meet their quick turn-around requirements. In essence, I built a sustainable partnership, secured the account, and continued to manage our relationship with them. For that achievement, I earned a significant bonus and two-tier promotion.

Sales Training & Team Leadership

Question: As the textile industry has undergone massive changes, downsizings, and reorganizations over the past decade, it has become even more critical that new sales associates be able to hit the ground running. Do you have any experience in sales training and team leadership and, if so, can you highlight your most notable accomplishments in this area?

Your Response: Training, developing, and mentoring field sales professionals is an inherent part of my current responsibilities as Timberland's New Markets Sales Director. When I accepted the position two years ago, the division was in turmoil. The previous Sales Director had left with no notice and the sales team had operated without leadership for more than five months. Over the next two years, I recruited and trained 35 new field sales associates, designed an internal sales training program, introduced a sales incentive program, and provided strong strategic and tactical leadership. Today, 30 of my 35 new hires are ranked in the top 10% of the company and the division is now one of the most profitable in the corporation.

Strategic Marketing

Question: As we've discussed, our company has experienced phenomenal sales growth over the past four years. However, we're at a crossroads now, in need of a Sales and Marketing Director with strong strategic planning and strategic marketing skills. Do you have any specific experience in strategic market planning?

Your Response: In three of my last four positions, I have driven the strategic marketing function to include market research, competitive analysis, market planning, market positioning, marketing communications, and field marketing support. And, in each position, our revenues have grown as a direct result of my leadership in identifying and capturing new market opportunities. For example, I conceived and orchestrated the strategic marketing process that has led LEIX into the specialty consumer market and increased their revenues 32% over the past year. For Meyerson, I created and implemented the strategy that led the company's successful expansion into the Far Eastern markets and now generates millions in annual revenue.

Territory Management

Question: This position would entail managing sales efforts throughout the entire LA metro area. Have you ever been responsible for full territory management and is this a position for which you believe that you are prepared?

Your Response: To answer in one word - YES! With four years of field sales experience under my belt, I am now ready to accept a new level of responsibility as a Territory Manager. Do I believe I'm qualified? Another resounding yes! Why? Because I delivered double-digit sales growth in all four years, because I have trained more than 20 other field sales representatives for the company, and because I am a confident customer relationship manager. What's more, not only are my sales and customer skills strong, I am efficient, well organized, and able to multi-task on a routine basis. The combination of those qualifications is what will propel me to succeed as your new Territory Manager.

KeyWord Accomplishment Phrases for Interviews, Resumes, & Cover Letters

Account Management & Retention

- Promoted rapidly through a series of increasingly responsible, corporate-level sales and marketing positions based on consistently strong performance in account management and retention despite entrenched market competition.

Competitive Wins

- Realigned pricing and market positioning strategies for AT&T's global account base, increased competitive wins by 42%, and improved net profitability of each sales transaction by an average of 25%.

Customer Relationship Management

- Designed and led a series of in-house training programs on customer relationship management focusing on the acquisition, management, and retention of key account relationships throughout the pharmaceutical sector.

Multi-Channel Distribution

- Designed and put in place a multi-channel distribution network to facilitate the flow of products from NYC ports to J. Crew's 12 fulfillment centers throughout the Northeastern U.S. Moved over $500 million in product annually.

New Business Development

- Specialized in new business development in regions throughout Latin America where previous sales associates were unsuccessful in closing any sales. Without eight months, closed two major accounts for a first-year revenue stream of more than $400,000.

New Product Launch

- Launched 30 new products into specialty markets throughout the territory to capture first-to-market position. New product lines generated an additional $1.1 million in annual sales with a better than 22% profit margin.

Sales Negotiations

- Excelled in highly competitive sales negotiations, consistently winning against the competition 90% of the time.

Sales Training & Team Leadership

- Created a top-flight sales organization specializing in ethnic marketing. Recruited National Sales Manager for direct sales and established a solid nationwide broker network across all classes of trade. Team delivered an additional $12 million in annual sales.

Strategic Marketing

- Authored the corporate strategic marketing plan that served as the foundation for Kodak's double-digit revenue growth within the Asian market in 2001 and 2002.

Territory Management

- Managed a $2.4 million dollar territory with full responsibility for new product launch, product management, new business development, account management, sales negotiations, sales contracts, and product delivery/installation.

Your Personal KeyWord Toolkit

Use the space below to add in KeyWords and KeyWord Phrases from your own career in Sales & Marketing. Once you've done that, you'll want to do three more things essential to the success of your job search campaign.

1. Write KeyWord accomplishment phrases for each new KeyWord and KeyWord Phrase on your list. Then, use those words in your resume, cover letters, and interviews.

2. Write KeyWord interview responses to use when each of those KeyWord topics comes up. That way, you'll be instantly prepared with answers that effectively highlight your accomplishments, key projects, record of promotion, honors and awards, and other distinguishing aspects of your career.

3. Practice #1 and #2 above over and over! Although it certainly isn't necessary that you memorize each and every accomplishment and interview response, it is essential that the moment the topic comes up during an interview, you're immediately prepared to answer.

Your KeyWords & KeyWord Phrases:

Chapter 18

KeyWords for
Senior Managers & Executives

Top 10 KeyWords & KeyWord Phrases

Board of Director Relations
Corporate Development
Cross-Functional Team Leadership
Management Development & Leadership
Organizational Development
Policy & Procedure Development
Profit & Loss Management
Revenue & Profit Growth
ROI/ROE/ROA Improvement
Strategic Planning

KeyWord Interview Q&A

Board of Director Relations

Question: Working with our Board of Directors is a key responsibility of the President's position. Have you worked with Boards in the past and, if so, on what types of issues?

Your Response: Since promoted to the executive level six years ago, I have worked closely with the Board of Directors in several critical capacities and on several major projects. Most recently, I won the Board's support for a major expansion initiative that will fund Glaxo's launch into the South African market. Last year, I presented the company's new strategic plan to the Board, successfully responded to a host of objections and concerns, and won full approval. In addition, I have led annual Board meetings, participated in the selection of new Board members, and worked to build cooperative relationships that have served the company well.

Corporate Development

Question: We need a strong leader in this position…an individual who can take control and accelerate our corporate development function. What key functions have you managed that fall within the scope of corporate development?

Your Response: Setting the direction for corporate development is one of my primary functions as one of Home Depot's top management executives. Specifically, I am responsible for driving the strategic planning function, merger and acquisition activities, alliances and joint ventures, long-range market direction and positioning, and overall corporate growth. I am the perfect combination of strategist and tactician, able to identify opportunities, set the course of action, and then personally negotiate and close major transactions. The pace of our corporate development efforts over the past several years has been phenomenal as the company continues to grow at better than 20% annually. The only reason I'm considering your opportunity is the fact that it would allow me to devote 100% of my time to corporate development and expansion, an area that I thoroughly enjoy and in which I excel.

Cross-Functional Team Leadership

Question: Managing a cross-functional business team requires a unique blend of talents. What talents and qualifications do you bring to the position that demonstrate your ability to build and lead productive teams?

Your Response: Building and leading cross-functional teams is what I do best. Whether working to develop and strengthen an existing team, or restaffing an organization to meet changing demands, I have consistently demonstrated my ability to recruit and retain top performers. By creating a corporate culture that rewards individual and group contribution, I have created a workplace where people want to work and want to stay. At peak, I've led up to 14 managers and executives representing finance, human resources, sales, marketing, information technology, corporate administration, engineering, and manufacturing. In addition, I've introduced the company's first-ever team-building and leadership-building events, which have further solidified the strength of our management team and our entire workforce. Offer me the opportunity to lead your cross-functional team and I guarantee I'll deliver strong and sustainable results.

Management Development & Leadership

Question: What do you think are the primary success factors for developing and leading a top management team?

Your Response: First and foremost, I think it's having the right team, and that starts back at the beginning with recruitment. In order to achieve the long-term goal of a highly productive management team, the right people must be brought into the organization-people with the same work ethic and commitment to excellence, people with unique talents and expertise, and people able to communicate and work collaboratively. Once you've created the right culture with the right people, then provided them with clear organizational goals and objectives, you're well on your way. Teams comprised of such individuals require little motivation; rather, they require a leader who can make decisions and provide a road map to success.

Organizational Development

Question: We're most interested in a candidate with a wealth of experience in organizational development. Can you please address your experience in this area?

Your Response: As the Global Director of Human Resources for Microsoft, I am directly responsible for leading a diversity of organizational development initiatives. Obviously, with such a vast organization of employees worldwide, much of my efforts are focused on the design and development of OD programs; followed by direct implementation by management teams throughout the field. Recent projects I've orchestrated include a company-wide succession management program, a major shift in corporate culture and philosophy from sales-driven to service-driven, and the implementation of long-range OD plans for each independent business unit. The opportunities available within OD are vast and, thus, make it one of the most interesting and most complex of all corporate management functions.

Policy & Procedure Development

Question: Personally speaking, I've never been one who enjoyed the task for developing policies and procedures. I much prefer being on the action end of things, not the planning end. That's why I'm looking at bringing in a business partner who can focus on the internal operations and create the policies that will continue to support the company's growth. So, how will your experience complement that?

Your Response: I can already tell that we're going to be a great match, as I much prefer to lead the internal, behind-the-scenes management functions. And, in particular, I thoroughly enjoy developing corporate policies, procedures, systems, methodologies, and the like. I believe that no organization is any stronger than its internal mechanisms and, as such, my jobs have always focused on creating the infrastructure to support growth, expansion, and improved profitability. Some of my projects that might be of particular interest include developing a comprehensive policy and procedure manual for Johnson & Johnson's finance operations, creating procedures to guide all financial planning and analysis functions for Bayer, and designing internal policies to guide order processing and fulfillment for Pfizer. Each and every project I undertake is intended to achieve either one of two purposes - improve operations and, in turn, profitability, or enhance the ways in which the business operates.

Profit & Loss Management

Question: For how many years have you held direct profit and loss responsibility? And can you share some results?

Your Response: I've held bottom-line P&L responsibility since 1998, when I was promoted to Regional Sales Manager. In this position for two years, I increased profitability 18%. Next, as U.S. Business Manager, I was responsible for the P&L performance of a $38 million enterprise. We experienced year-over-year revenue growth of 22% and improved profits an average of 16% annually. Now, as President of Sony's U.S. operations, I have full P&L for a $1.2 billion operation with 218 stores and 2,000-plus employees. Most important, I've exceeded annual profit goals by 28% in 2002 and 19% in 2003, with projections for an additional 12% by year-end 2004.

Revenue & Profit Growth

Question: Building revenues is one thing. Building profits is another. Have you been successful in both endeavors and, if so, how?

Your Response: Let's start with my success in revenue growth. Under my leadership, Exxon's co-generation revenues have increased each year for the past eight consecutive years. Average revenue growth has been 7% to 8% annually, with one year closing at 14%. This growth is primarily attributable to my personal successes in sales and contract negotiations with our key customer base. Regarding profits, performance has been even stronger as a result of several key cost-cutting initiatives that my team and I implemented. When I assumed P&L responsibility for the plant, it was operating at about a 12% profit margin. Now, eight years later, our profit averages 22% to 24% annually.

ROI/ROE/ROA Improvement

Question: Now that our new Board and President are in place, I'm ready to begin transitioning out of the organization. However, I promised to recruit a new CFO prior to leaving and ensure his or her full assimilation into the organization. One of the factors most important in that decision is a candidate's ability to improve all financial returns to the company and to our stockholders. Please address your experience in improving ROI, ROE, and ROA.

Your Response: As a CFO, I consider it my primary responsibility to improve our financial returns. Working in cooperation with the President, Sales Manager, and Operations Manager at Siemens U.S., we've delivered phenomenal financial results. ROI has improved 27%, ROE 32%, and ROA 18%, just over the past three years. This has been accomplished through better financial leadership and controls, improved operating leadership, an intense focus on increasing sales in the right markets, and a strategic approach to business growth and development. Our future financial projections are just as strong and will continue to position the company as one of the industry's brightest performers. The only reason I'm considering leaving the company is my desire to relocate to Manhattan so that my wife can continue in her career and my son can attend NYU.

Strategic Planning

Question: How much of your time and effort is focused on strategic planning?

Your Response: A good estimate of my time devoted to strategic planning would be 35%, most of which occurs over a three-month period each year when the Chairman of the Board and I orchestrate our annual strategic planning process for the company and all of its operating divisions worldwide. Working in cooperation with top executives and managers throughout the company, we are the ones responsible for defining and refining long-term strategic direction, guiding corporate development activities, and ensuring that we have the appropriate financial, human, and operating resources to meet our objectives. Although others may consider this a less-than-exciting responsibility, I thoroughly enjoy the challenge of putting all the pieces together and using my analytical and planning skills in tandem with my operating experience. What's more, I personally author employee memoranda and lead employee conferences to ensure that we are effectively communicating our plans and objectives to the workforce, where the end results will truly happen.

KeyWord Accomplishment Phrases for Interviews, Resumes, & Cover Letters

Board of Director Relations

■ Appointed to the Board of Directors of six companies acquired by the Smith Barney Venture Capital Fund to represent the firm's financial stake in each of these acquisitions. In each situation, established and maintained outstanding working relationships with all key Board members.

Corporate Development

■ Championed a series of corporate development projects involving three mergers, two acquisitions, two divestitures, and a worldwide sales and marketing expansion project. Total financial investment exceeded $850 million.

Cross-Functional Team Leadership

■ Excelled in the development and leadership of cross-functional project management teams leading corporate initiatives in policy development, regulatory affairs, corporate legal affairs, corporate administration, and long-term strategic planning and growth.

Management Development & Leadership

- Hand-selected top candidates to complete Harvard's management development and leadership training program in a direct effort to encourage the retention of employees being fast-tracked to top management positions within the organization.

Organizational Development

- Spearheaded a portfolio of organizational development initiatives incorporating culture change, process redesign, workforce development, technology acquisition, and performance metrics as Shell Oil underwent three major downsizings and a global market repositioning.

Policy & Procedure Development

- Authored corporate policies and procedures governing the issuance of corporate bonds, mutual funds, and other consumer investment products to ensure full protection of the corporation, a competitive advantage in the marketplace, and solid financial returns to investors, partners, and lenders.

Profit & Loss Management

- Appointed General Manager of McCormick's Latin American Division with full profit and loss responsibility for the entire $200 million organization. Achieved and sustained double-digit profitability for 12 consecutive years despite an intensely competitive and volatile market.

Revenue & Profit Growth

- Exceeded all revenue and profit growth goals as established by the Board of Directors. Increased domestic revenues 24% and profits 34%; increased international revenues 35% and profits 22%.

ROI/ROE/ROA Improvement

- After just one year as the President & CEO of Matrix Electronics, improved ROI 22%, ROE 18%, and ROA 8% with no additional financial investment in the company.

Strategic Planning

- Credited with guiding the strategic planning process that redefined Heinhold's position in the agricultural market as a company well-respected for its forward thinking and action in capturing emerging opportunities and generating profitable returns.

Your Personal KeyWord Toolkit

Use the space below to add in KeyWords and KeyWord Phrases from your own career as a Senior Manager & Executive. Once you've done that, you'll want to do three more things essential to the success of your job search campaign.

1. Write KeyWord accomplishment phrases for each new KeyWord and KeyWord Phrase on your list. Then, use those words in your resume, cover letters, and interviews.

2. Write KeyWord interview responses to use when each of those KeyWord topics comes up. That way, you'll be instantly prepared with answers that effectively highlight your accomplishments, key projects, record of promotion, honors and awards, and other distinguishing aspects of your career.

3. Practice #1 and #2 above over and over! Although it certainly isn't necessary that you memorize each and every accomplishment and interview response, it is essential that the moment the topic comes up during an interview, you're immediately prepared to answer.

Your KeyWords & KeyWord Phrases:

_____

_____

_____

_____

_____

_____

_____

Chapter 19

KeyWords for the
Technology Professional

Top 10 KeyWords & KeyWord Phrases

E-commerce
Information Systems Management
Internet Technology
Multimedia Technologies
Networking Technology
Next-Generation Technology
Systems & Applications
Technology Commercialization
Technology Transfers & Licensing
User Training & Support

KeyWord Interview Q&A

E-commerce

Question: As with many other major retailers, we are now looking to transition a large bulk of our sales to an e-commerce platform. How involved were you in establishing Barnes & Noble's e-commerce capabilities?

Your Response: The Executive Vice President of Technology at Barnes & Noble recruited me directly because of my background in designing and implementing e-commerce technologies for several other retail organizations. These included Sears, Hallmark, Macy's, and Tru-Value, to name just a few. Brought in at the earliest of planning stages, I spearheaded the development of B&N's entire e-commerce operations which now generate sales in excess of $800 million annually. Briefly summarized, I selected the hardware and software, led the applications and Web development teams, defined the e-commerce transactions protocol, and guided the project from concept to full-scale implementation within nine months. It was a huge effort that involved more than 50 personnel, yet we were able to recover our development costs in less than six months of operation. Now, we are working on the next-generation e-commerce applications to further streamline customer usability and encourage increased sales.

Information Systems Management

Question: In looking for the right candidate to assume management responsibility for our IS department, we've decided that we're most interested in an individual who has risen through the ranks to his or her current management assignment. We believe this gives the individual a unique perspective as to what is involved in managing such a diverse operation. Can you please detail your career background?

Your Response: My career track is straightforward. I was recruited by Baltimore Gas & Electric immediately following graduation from the University of Baltimore and have remained with the company for the past 18 years. Starting as a Programmer, I advanced to Senior Programmer, Associate Project Manager, Senior Project Manager, IS Team Leader, and now my current position as Associate Manager of the entire IS operation. This is a 24/7 operation with more than 3,500 users on a daily basis accessing our systems and networks from locations throughout the state. Currently, I lead a staff of 32 programmers and project managers, and control an annual operating budget of $3.8 million. My career has been one of cumulative responsibilities, just as you're looking for. Beginning with a hands-on role and retaining that hands-on responsibility for years and years, I rose through the management ranks and am now poised for the #1 IS management position.

Internet Technology

Question: When I received your request to be promoted to direct the development of our Internet Web presence, I must say that I was surprised. In fact, I had no idea that you had any interest in technology since it certainly isn't a major part of your current job responsibilities with us. As such, what makes you qualified for this position?

Your Response: I've always enjoyed technology and been an avid PC user long before most people even knew what PC stood for! Then, about six years ago, just as the Internet was beginning to really penetrate the commercial market, I began developing websites for friends, family, and small businesses in the area. Little did I know that word would get out that Internet technology was my expertise, but it did. Now, six years later, I've designed more than 200 websites, from simple one-page sites to complex, multi-layer sites with 100-plus pages. In fact, I've outlined on this page what I consider to be some of my best work and hope that you will take the time to visit some of these sites where you can get a sense of my skills in site design, functionality, and usability. Once you've seen them, I'm sure you'll be confident that I can manage your Internet development project.

Multimedia Technologies

Question: Creating multimedia technologies for the educational market is the primary responsibility of this position. As such, I would be most interested in any related professional experience you may have.

Your Response: As an Instructional Technologist with the Cambridge Public School District, I have led the development of a large portfolio of multimedia technologies to support classroom learning. Specifically, I've designed both Internet and Intranet sites for the District, implemented networks, created online instructional programs, installed scores of software programs and new applications, and designed CD-based educational modules. Just as important, I've worked hand-in-hand with classroom teachers, media specialists, and school administrators to define their needs for instructional technologies and ensure that our deliverables were in line with their expectations and student capabilities. Having the opportunity to work for a technology development company such as yours is the next step in my career, allowing me to transfer what I've learned in the field into your R&D organization.

Networking Technology

Question: When networking first came into vogue, customers were thrilled
                     to just have the basic technology to make the connection hap-
                     pen. Over the years, however, with the constant growth within
                     the industry, our customers have come to expect so much more
                     and we need a distinct market advantage. How can you help
                     us?

Your Response: I believe that networking is not just about the technology or the
                     application, but about the users and how we, as a company, can
                     respond to their specific needs. This can be difficult, knowing
                     that each customer has unique requirements and a one-size-
                     fits-all solution simply does not work. Therefore, the focus must
                     be on customization of each network that we sell. We must fully
                     understand the user's needs and application requirements, and
                     deliver a system that meets those needs today and in the future.
                     If we can build these types of relationships, where our custom-
                     ers know that we truly understand their needs and will respond,
                     then we have instantly halted our competition in their tracks
                     and won the confidence and trust of our customers. This will
                     allow us to then position ourselves as the premier provider of
                     networking technology for any and every solution.

Next-Generation Technology

Question: Hidden away, in the depths of our corporate complex, is a small
                     R&D department that, with only 12 employees, leads the devel-
                     opment of all of our next-generation technologies, systems, and
                     applications. It's a wonderful place to work and we have virtu-
                     ally no turnover. The only reason we have an opening at this
                     time is that one of our engineers relocated to Southern Califor-
                     nia. What is the greatest asset you bring to this unique organi-
                     zation?

Your Response: First of all, the environment sounds wonderful. It's not often
                     that individuals like myself have the opportunity to work hand-
                     in-hand with some of the nation's leading technology develop-
                     ment experts. Frankly, I'm honored just to be interviewed! Now,
                     when you ask about my greatest asset, it is undoubtedly my
                     ability to fast-track projects through development. In my eight
                     years with Microsoft, I was actively involved in the develop-
                     ment of scores of next-generation products and am proud to say

that all projects under my leadership were either delivered on or ahead of schedule. This includes several releases of Microsoft Office, one of which I finished three months before the deadline and $550,000 under budget. Once I'm up to speed on your specific development projects, I will work diligently to deliver the same type of results while never forfeiting the quality, reliability, or integrity of your products.

Systems & Applications

Question: A job in systems and applications design is not one of the most glamorous in our company. It's a lot of hard work, long hours, and detail. What do you believe makes you most qualified for our systems engineering position when the bulk of your experience has been in field engineering?

Your Response: My current position requires two distinct skill sets. First, I must be a well-trained and capable engineer, able to quickly diagnose system and application problems, implement corrective actions, and bring the system back up to full-scale operation. The second skill is constant customer interaction which, although I have performed well, is not what I enjoy doing. I much prefer the work associated with systems troubleshooting, problem isolation, and repair. Knowing that my long-term career goal was to work in systems engineering, I have studied systems and applications design for the past two years, just earning my Associate of Arts degree last month. As such, I believe that the combination of my technical field experience and my strong technical training has positioned me well for a systems design position and I would be delighted if it could be with your company.

Technology Commercialization

Question: I must admit you've had a most unique career path in comparison to our other candidates, all of whom come from corporate America. To be honest, we'd never thought of looking to a university for a candidate. However, I'm impressed with what I read about your technology commercialization experience and would like to know more.

Your Response: One of the greatest advantages of working in academia has been the opportunity to work with so many technology leaders - Microsoft, Sony, Dell, Nokia, Symantec - the list goes on and on.

Partnering with these companies to develop and then commercialize their new technologies is what I've devoted the past 15 years of my career to and what I will continue to do. Working on the leading edge is a great place to be and allows me to use my unique combination of skills in technology design, engineering, and development, along with my uncanny ability to predict future technology trends, applications, and user demands. Most notable is the diversity of technology with which I have worked, from wireless cable to HDTV, from satellite communications to MP3 applications. As your Director of New Technology Development, I guarantee I'll continue to deliver innovation, excellence, and strong financial results.

Technology Transfers & Licensing

Question: Our business development team focuses primarily on structuring and negotiating technology transfers and licenses throughout the Far Eastern market. Do you have any experience in that market? What about in negotiating technology agreements?

Your Response: The answer to both of your questions is yes. Let me explain. In my current position with Ericsson, I travel worldwide to identify new business opportunities for the sharing, transfer, licensing, and commercialization of telecommunications technologies. Over the past five years, I have personally structured, negotiated, and transacted more than 50 such agreements with technology partners in Korea, Japan, China, Sri Lanka, Australia, and New Zealand, in addition to several European countries. In fact, since much of our business is in China, I have been studying Mandarin Chinese for the past two years. Although certainly not fluent, I can hold a casual conversation, which has been remarkably impressive to my Chinese business partners.

User Training & Support

Question: The hiring committee is most interested in a Software Development Manager who has a wealth of experience in user training and support. Has this been a function for which you've been responsible?

Your Response: With more than 10 years' experience in software development and engineering, one of my principal responsibilities has been the implementation of new software throughout the Kellogg organization. Inherent in that function was the on-site training of all headquarters personnel and the training of the field team responsible for on-site implementation at more than 200 Kellogg facilities worldwide. In addition, I currently oversee the operations of the user help desk organization which supports more than 5,000 Kellogg personnel in more than 50 countries. So, yes, I have substantial experience in user training and support.

KeyWord Accomplishment Phrases for Interviews, Resumes, & Cover Letters

E-commerce

- Led Tupperware's entrance into the e-commerce market, now a $2 billion revenue stream for the corporation with $2.8 billion forecasted for 2004.

Information Systems Management

- Directed a 24-person Information Systems Management Department for Appalachian Electric Power during a period of massive expansion. Led more than 20 system upgrades and enhancements to further expedite field and customer service operations.

Internet Technology

- One of the first in the history of the retail industry to introduce Internet technology into the corporation in a direct effort to transition a minimum of 20% of total sales from store-based to Web-based. As a result, reduced cost of sales by an average of 8% on all key product lines.

Multimedia Technologies

- Created a portfolio of multimedia technologies to supplement Nationwide's reliance on traditional marketing and customer development activities. Integrated e-mail prospecting, a massive Internet presence, PowerPoint corporate sales presentations, laptop sales tracking, and teleconferencing capabilities, resulting in 20% customer growth and 30% revenue growth.

Networking Technology

- Lead Engineer and Project Manager orchestrating the development and market launch of Sysco's networking technology undertaken in an effort to retain the company's strong market position. Successful effort recaptured lost customers and strengthened current customer relationships with new networking technologies.

Next-Generation Technology

- Member of six-person R&D team tasked with conceiving and developing next-generation PC technology on behalf of Bill Gates and the entire Microsoft organization.

Systems & Applications

- As Project Manager with Digital Equipment, led the development and implementation of scores of new technology systems and user applications for worldwide sale throughout both corporate and consumer markets. To date, led teams responsible for development and deployment of six major new systems that now generate over $500 million in annual sales.

Technology Commercialization

- Structured, negotiated, and transacted four technology commercialization agreements between Arizona State University's Technology Center and Panasonic for the market launch of next-generation voice-activated computer technology.

Technology Transfers & Licensing

- Identified opportunities and negotiated over $650 million in technology transfer and licensing agreements between U.S. technology companies and emerging enterprises throughout the African continent.

User Training & Support

- Revitalized the entire user training and support organization at Redken's corporate headquarters to ensure full utilization of new technologies. Documented measurable gains in productivity and efficiency, while eliminating repetitive functions and better utilizing staff competencies.

Your Personal KeyWord Toolkit

Use the space on the next page to add in KeyWords and KeyWord Phrases from your own career in Technology. Once you've done that, you'll want to do three more things essential to the success of your job search campaign.

1. Write KeyWord accomplishment phrases for each new KeyWord and KeyWord Phrase on your list. Then, use those words in your resume, cover letters, and interviews.

2. Write KeyWord interview responses to use when each of those KeyWord topics comes up. That way, you'll be instantly prepared with answers that effectively highlight your accomplishments, key projects, record of promotion, honors and awards, and other distinguishing aspects of your career.

3. Practice #1 and #2 above over and over! Although it certainly isn't necessary that you memorize each and every accomplishment and interview response, it is essential that the moment the topic comes up during an interview, you're immediately prepared to answer.

Your KeyWords & KeyWord Phrases:

_____

_____

_____

_____

_____

_____

_____

_____

_____

Chapter 20

Action Verbs,
High-Impact Phrases,
and Personality Descriptors

Review the following lists of Action Verbs, High-Impact Phrases, and Personality Descriptors, select those that accurately reflect you and your experience, and then use them in your interviews, resumes, and cover letters. They'll liven up your conversation and your written words!

Review the following lists of Action Verbs, High-Impact Phrases, and Personality Descriptors, select those that accurately reflect you and your experience, and then integrate them into the text of your resume and cover letters.

Action Verbs

Accelerate	Arrange	Chart	Conclude
Accomplish	Ascertain	Clarify	Conduct
Achieve	Assemble	Classify	Conserve
Acquire	Assess	Close	Consolidate
Adapt	Assist	Coach	Construct
Address	Author	Collect	Consult
Advance	Authorize	Command	Continue
Advise	Brief	Communicate	Contract
Advocate	Budget	Compare	Convert
Analyze	Build	Compel	Coordinate
Apply	Calculate	Compile	Correct
Appoint	Capture	Complete	Counsel
Arbitrate	Catalog	Compute	Craft
Architect	Champion	Conceive	Create

Critique
Decrease
Define
Delegate
Deliver
Demonstrate
Deploy
Design
Detail
Detect
Determine
Develop
Devise
Direct
Discover
Dispense
Display
Distribute
Diversify
Divert
Document
Double
Draft
Drive
Earn
Edit
Educate
Effect
Elect
Eliminate
Emphasize
Enact
Encourage
Endure
Energize
Enforce
Engineer
Enhance
Enlist
Ensure
Establish

Estimate
Evaluate
Examine
Exceed
Execute
Exhibit
Expand
Expedite
Experiment
Export
Facilitate
Finalize
Finance
Forge
Form
Formalize
Formulate
Found
Generate
Govern
Graduate
Guide
Halt
Head
Hire
Honor
Hypothesize
Identify
Illustrate
Imagine
Implement
Import
Improve
Improvise
Increase
Influence
Inform
Initiate
Innovate
Inspect
Inspire

Install
Institute
Instruct
Integrate
Intensify
Interpret
Interview
Introduce
Invent
Inventory
Investigate
Judge
Justify
Launch
Lead
Lecture
License
Listen
Locate
Maintain
Manage
Manipulate
Manufacture
Map
Market
Mastermind
Measure
Mediate
Mentor
Model
Modify
Monitor
Motivate
Navigate
Negotiate
Nominate
Normalize
Observe
Obtain
Offer
Officiate

Operate
Orchestrate
Organize
Orient
Originate
Outsource
Overcome
Oversee
Participate
Perceive
Perfect
Perform
Persuade
Pilot
Pinpoint
Pioneer
Plan
Position
Predict
Prepare
Prescribe
Present
Preside
Process
Procure
Program
Progress
Project
Project manage
Promote
Propose
Prospect
Provide
Publicize
Purchase
Qualify
Question
Rate
Realign
Rebuild
Recapture

Receive
Recognize
Recommend
Reconcile
Record
Recruit
Redesign
Reduce
Reengineer
Regain
Regulate
Rehabilitate
Reinforce
Rejuvenate
Render
Renegotiate
Reorganize
Report
Reposition
Represent
Research
Resolve
Respond
Restore
Restructure
Retrieve
Review
Revise
Revitalize
Satisfy
Schedule
Secure
Select
Separate
Serve
Simplify
Sold
Solidify
Solve
Speak
Specify

Standardize
Stimulate
Streamline
Structure
Succeed
Suggest
Summarize
Supervise
Supply
Support
Surpass
Synthesize
Systematize
Tabulate
Target
Teach
Terminate
Test
Thwart
Train
Transcribe
Transfer
Transform
Transition
Translate
Troubleshoot
Unify
Unite
Update
Upgrade
Use
Utilize
Verbalize
Verify
Win
Write

High-Impact Phrases

Accelerated Career Track
Accelerating Revenue Growth
Aggressive Turnaround Leadership
Benchmarking
Best in Class
Business Process Redesign
Business Process Reengineering
Capturing Cost Reductions
Catalyst for Change
Change Agent
Change Management
Competitive Market Positioning
Competitive Wins
Competitively Positioning Products & Technologies
Contemporary Management Style
Core Competencies
Creative Business Leader
Creative Problem Solver
Cross-Culturally Sensitive
Cross-Functional Expertise
Cross-Functional Team Leadership
Decisive Management Style
Delivering Strong and Sustainable Gains
Direct & Decisive Organizational Leadership
Distinguished Performance
Driving Customer Loyalty Initiatives
Driving Innovation
Driving Performance Improvement
Driving Productivity Gains
Emerging Business Ventures
Emerging International Markets
Entrepreneurial Drive
Entrepreneurial Leadership
Entrepreneurial Vision
Executive Leadership
Executive Liaison
Fast-Track Promotion
Global Market Dominance
High-Caliber

High-Growth
High-Impact
High-Performance
High-Quality
Matrix Management
Multi-Discipline Industry Expertise
Organizational Driver
Organizational Leader
Outperforming Global Competition
Outperforming Market Competition
PC Proficient
Peak Performer
Performance Improvement
Performance Management
Performance Reengineering
Pioneering Technologies
Proactive Business Leader
Proactive Manager
Process Redesign
Process Reengineering
Productivity Improvement
Self-Starter
Start-Up, Turnaround, & High-Growth Organizations
Strategic & Tactical Operations
Strong & Sustainable Financial Gains
Strong & Sustainable Performance Gains
Strong & Sustainable Productivity Gains
Strong & Sustainable Profit Gains
Strong & Sustainable Quality Gains
Strong & Sustainable Technology Gains
Team Building
Team Leadership
Technologically Advanced Organization
Technologically Sophisticated Operations
Top Flight Leadership Competencies
Top Tier Executive
Visionary Leadership
World Class Leadership
World Class Operations
World Class Organization

Personality Descriptors

Abstract
Accurate
Action-Driven
Adaptable
Adventurous
Aggressive
Amenable
Analytical
Artful
Assertive
Believable
Bilingual
Bold
Brave
Communicative
Competent
Competitive
Conceptual
Confident
Conscientious
Conservative
Cooperative
Courageous
Creative
Credible
Cross-Cultural
Culturally Sensitive
Customer-Driven
Dauntless
Decisive
Dedicated
Dependable
Determined
Devoted
Diligent
Diplomatic
Direct
Dramatic
Driven
Dynamic

Eager
Earnest
Effective
Efficient
Eloquent
Employee-Driven
Empowered
Encouraging
Energetic
Energized
Enterprising
Enthusiastic
Entrepreneurial
Ethical
Experienced
Expert
Expressive
Forward-Thinking
Global
Hardworking
Healthy
Helpful
Heroic
High-Impact
High-Potential
Honest
Honorable
Humanistic
Humanitarian
Humorous
Immediate
Impactful
Important
Impressive
Incomparable
Independent
Individualistic
Industrious
Ingenious

Innovative
Insightful
Intelligent
Intense
Intuitive
Judicious
Keen
Leader
Loyal
Managerial
Market-Driven
Masterful
Mature
Mechanical
Methodical
Modern
Moral
Motivated
Motivational
Multilingual
Notable
Noteworthy
Objective
Observant
Opportunistic
Oratorical
Orderly
Organized
Outstanding
Participative
Participatory
Peerless
Perfectionist
Performance-Driven
Persevering
Persistent
Personable
Persuasive
Philosophical

Photogenic
Pioneering
Poised
Polished
Popular
Positive
Practical
Pragmatic
Precise
Preeminent
Prepared
Proactive
Problem Solver
Productive
Professional
Proficient
Progressive
Prominent
Prudent
Punctual
Quality-Driven
Reactive
Reliable
Reputable
Resilient
Resourceful
Results-Driven
Results-Oriented
Savvy
Sensitive
Sharp
Skilled
Skillful
Sophisticated
Spirited
Strategic
Strong
Subjective
Successful
Tactful
Talented

Teacher
Team Builder
Team Leader
Team Player
Technical
Tenacious
Thorough
Tolerant
Top Performer
Top Producer
Traditional
Trainer
Trilingual
Trouble Shooter
Trustworthy
Truthful
Understanding
Unrelenting
Upbeat
Valiant
Valuable
Venturesome
Veracious
Verbal
Victorious
Vigorous
Virtuous
Visionary
Vital
Vivacious
Well-Balanced
Well-Versed
Winning
Wise
Worldly
Youthful
Zealous
Zestful

Career Resources

THE FOLLOWING CAREER RESOURCES are available directly from Impact Publications. Full descriptions of each title as well as nine downloadable catalogs, videos, and software can be found on our website: www.impactpublications.com. Complete the following form or list the titles, include shipping (see formula at the end), enclose payment, and send your order to:

IMPACT PUBLICATIONS
9104 Manassas Drive, Suite N
Manassas Park, VA 20111-5211 USA
1-800-361-1055 (orders only)
Tel. 703-361-7300 or Fax 703-335-9486
Email address: info@impactpublications.com
Quick & easy online ordering: www.impactpublications.com

Orders from individuals must be prepaid by check, money order, or major credit card. We accept telephone, fax, and email orders.

Qty.	TITLES	Price	TOTAL
Books By Wendy S. Enelow			
____	101 Ways to Recession-Proof Your Career	14.95	_____
____	Best KeyWords for Resumes, Cover Letters, and Interviews	14.95	_____
____	Best Cover Letters for $100,000+ Jobs	24.95	_____
____	Best Resumes and CVs for International Jobs	24.95	_____
____	Best Resumes for $100,000+ Jobs	24.95	_____
____	Best Resumes for People Without a Four-Year Degree	19.95	_____
____	Cover Letter Magic	16.95	_____
____	Expert Resumes for Computer and Web Jobs	16.95	_____
____	Expert Resumes for Managers and Executives	16.95	_____
____	Expert Resumes for Manufacturing Careers	16.95	_____
____	Expert Resumes for People Returning to Work	16.95	_____
____	Expert Resumes for Teachers and Educators	16.95	_____
____	KeyWords to Nail Your Job Interview	17.95	_____
____	Winning Interviews for $100,000+ Jobs	17.95	_____

Changing Addictive and Not-So-Hot Behaviors

_____	Angry Men	14.95	_____
_____	Angry Women	14.95	_____
_____	Denial Is Not a River in Egypt	11.95	_____
_____	If Life Is a Game, These Are the Rules	15.00	_____
_____	If Success Is a Game, These Are the Rules	17.50	_____
_____	No One Is Unemployable	29.95	_____
_____	No One Will Hire Me!	13.95	_____
_____	Passages Through Recovery	14.00	_____
_____	Sex, Drugs, Gambling and Chocolate	15.95	_____
_____	Stop the Chaos	12.95	_____
_____	The Truth About Addiction and Recovery	14.00	_____
_____	Understanding the Twelve Steps	12.00	_____
_____	You Can Heal Your Life	17.95	_____

Attitude and Motivation

_____	100 Ways to Motivate Yourself	18.99	_____
_____	Change Your Attitude	15.99	
_____	Reinventing Yourself	18.99	_____

Inspiration and Empowerment

_____	101 Secrets of Highly Effective Speakers	15.95	_____
_____	Do What You Love for the Rest of Your Life	24.95	_____
_____	Dream It Do It	16.95	_____
_____	Life Strategies	13.95	_____
_____	Power of Purpose	20.00	_____
_____	Practical Dreamer's Handbook	13.95	_____
_____	Self Matters	14.00	_____
_____	Seven Habits of Highly Effective People	14.00	_____
_____	Who Moved My Cheese?	19.95	_____

Testing and Assessment

_____	Career Tests	12.95	_____
_____	Discover the Best Jobs for You	15.95	_____
_____	Discover What You're Best At	14.00	_____
_____	Do What You Are	18.95	_____
_____	Finding Your Perfect Work	16.95	_____
_____	I Could Do Anything If Only I Knew What It Was	13.95	_____
_____	I Want to Do Something Else, But I'm Not Sure What It Is	15.95	_____
_____	Now, Discover Your Strengths	27.00	_____
_____	Pathfinder	14.00	_____
_____	What Should I Do With My Life?	24.95	_____
_____	What Type Am I?	14.95	_____
_____	What's Your Type of Career?	17.95	_____

Career Exploration and Job Strategies

_____	5 Patterns of Extraordinary Careers	17.95	_____
_____	25 Jobs That Have It All	12.95	_____
_____	50 Cutting Edge Jobs	15.95	_____

____ 95 Mistakes Job Seekers Make and		
How to Avoid Them	13.95	_____
____ 100 Great Jobs and How to Get Them	17.95	_____
____ 101 Ways to Recession-Proof Your Career	14.95	_____
____ America's Top 100 Jobs for People		
Without a Four-Year Degree	19.95	_____
____ Best Jobs for the 21st Century	19.95	_____
____ Career Change	14.95	_____
____ Career Intelligence	15.95	_____
____ Change Your Job, Change Your Life		
(9th Edition)	21.95	_____
____ Cool Careers for Dummies	19.99	_____
____ Directory of Executive Recruiters	49.95	_____
____ Five Secrets to Finding a Job	12.95	_____
____ Haldane's Best Secrets of the		
Hidden Job Market	15.95	_____
____ High-Tech Careers for Low-Tech People	14.95	_____
____ How to Get a Job and Keep It	16.95	_____
____ How to Succeed Without a Career Path	13.95	_____
____ Job Hunting Guide: Transitioning		
From College to Career	14.95	_____
____ Knock 'Em Dead	14.95	_____
____ Me, Myself, and I, Inc.	17.95	_____
____ Occupational Outlook Handbook	18.95	_____
____ O*NET Dictionary of Occupational Titles	39.95	_____
____ Quit Your Job and Grow Some Hair	15.95	_____
____ Rites of Passage at $100,000 to $1 Million+	29.95	_____
____ What Color Is Your Parachute?	17.95	_____
____ Working Identify	26.95	_____

Internet Job Search

____ 100 Top Internet Job Sites	12.95	_____
____ America's Top Internet Job Sites	19.95	_____
____ CareerXroads (annual)	26.95	_____
____ Career Exploration On the Internet	24.95	_____
____ Cyberspace Job Search Kit	18.95	_____
____ Directory of Websites for International Jobs	19.95	_____
____ Guide to Internet Job Searching	14.95	_____
____ Haldane's Best Employment Websites		
for Professionals	15.95	_____
____ Job Search Online for Dummies		
(with CD-ROM)	24.99	_____

Resumes and Letters

____ 101 Great Tips for a Dynamite Resume	13.95	_____
____ 175 Best Cover Letters	14.95	_____
____ 201 Dynamite Job Search Letters	19.95	_____
____ America's Top Resumes for America's		
Top Jobs	19.95	_____
____ Best KeyWords for Resumes,		
Cover Letters, & Interviews	17.95	_____

____ Best Resumes and CVs for International Jobs	24.95	_____
____ Best Resumes for $100,000+ Jobs	24.95	_____
____ Best Resumes for People Without a Four-Year Degree	19.95	_____
____ Best Cover Letters for $100,000+ Jobs	24.95	_____
____ Cover Letters for Dummies	16.99	_____
____ Cover Letters That Knock 'Em Dead	12.95	_____
____ Cyberspace Resume Kit	18.95	_____
____ Dynamite Cover Letters	14.95	_____
____ Dynamite Resumes	14.95	_____
____ e-Resumes	14.95	_____
____ Gallery of Best Cover Letters	18.95	_____
____ Gallery of Best Resumes	18.95	_____
____ Haldane's Best Cover Letters for Professionals	15.95	_____
____ Haldane's Best Resumes for Professionals	15.95	_____
____ High Impact Resumes and Letters	19.95	_____
____ Resume Shortcuts	14.95	_____
____ Resumes for Dummies	16.99	_____
____ Resumes for the Health Care Professional	14.95	_____
____ Resumes in Cyberspace	14.95	_____
____ Resumes That Knock 'Em Dead	12.95	_____
____ The Savvy Resume Writer	12.95	_____
____ Sure-Hire Resumes	14.95	_____

Networking

____ Dynamite Telesearch	12.95	_____
____ A Foot in the Door	14.95	_____
____ Golden Rule of Schmoozing	12.95	_____
____ Great Connections	11.95	_____
____ How to Work a Room	14.00	_____
____ Masters of Networking	16.95	_____
____ Power Networking	14.95	_____
____ The Savvy Networker	13.95	_____

Dress, Image, and Etiquette

____ Dressing Smart for Men	16.95	_____
____ Dressing Smart for Women	16.95	_____
____ Power Etiquette	14.95	_____
____ Professional Impressions	14.95	_____

Interviews

____ 101 Dynamite Questions to Ask At Your Job Interview	13.95	_____
____ Haldane's Best Answers to Tough Interview Questions	15.95	_____
____ Interview for Success	15.95	_____
____ Job Interview Tips for People With Not-So-Hot Backgrounds	14.95	_____
____ Job Interviews for Dummies	16.99	_____
____ KeyWords to Nail Your Job Interview	17.95	_____
____ Nail the Job Interview!	13.95	_____

____	The Savvy Interviewer	10.95	_____

Salary Negotiations

____	Better Than Money	18.95	_____
____	Dynamite Salary Negotiations	15.95	_____
____	Get a Raise in 7 Days	14.95	_____
____	Haldane's Best Salary Tips for Professionals	15.95	_____

Military in Transition

____	Jobs and the Military Spouse	17.95	_____
____	Military Resumes and Cover Letters	21.95	_____

Ex-Offenders in Transition

____	9 to 5 Beats Ten to Life	15.00	_____
____	99 Days and a Get Up	9.95	_____
____	Ex-Offender's Job Search Companion	9.95	_____
____	Man, I Need a Job	7.95	_____
____	Putting the Bars Behind You (6 books)	64.70	_____

Government and Nonprofit Jobs

____	Complete Guide to Public Employment	19.95	_____
____	Federal Applications That Get Results	23.95	_____
____	Federal Employment From A to Z	14.50	_____
____	FBI Careers	18.95	_____
____	Find a Federal Job Fast!	15.95	_____
____	Jobs and Careers With Nonprofit Organizations	17.95	_____
____	Ten Steps to a Federal Job	39.95	_____

International and Travel Jobs

____	Back Door Guide to Short-Term Job Adventures	21.95	_____
____	Inside Secrets to Finding a Career in Travel	14.95	_____
____	International Jobs	19.00	_____
____	International Job Finder	19.95	_____
____	Jobs for Travel Lovers	17.95	_____
____	Teaching English Abroad	15.95	_____
____	Work Your Way Around the World	17.95	_____

VIDEOS

Video Series

____	50 Best Jobs for the 21st Century	545.00	_____
____	60- Minute Self-Renewal Video Series	1999.95	_____
____	Job Finding for People With Disabilities Video Series	199.95	_____
____	Job Search Skills Video Series	799.00	_____
____	Job Success Without a College Degree Series	560.00	_____
____	Managing Your Personal Finances Series	499.00	_____
____	One Stop Career Center Video Series	599.00	_____
____	Portfolio Resumes Series	150.00	_____
____	Quick Job Search Video Series	545.00	_____
____	Road to Re-Employment Video Series	219.95	_____

____ Welfare-to-Work Video Series	545.00	_____
____ Work Maturity Skills Video Series	799.00	_____

Individual Videos

Interview, Networking, and Salary Videos

____ Build a Network for Work and Life	129.00	_____
____ Common Mistakes People Make in Interviews	79.95	_____
____ Exceptional Interviewing Tips	79.00	_____
____ Extraordinary Answers to Interview Questions	79.95	_____
____ Extreme Interview	69.00	_____
____ Make a First Good Impression	129.00	_____
____ Mastering the Interview	98.00	_____
____ Seizing the Job Interview	79.00	_____
____ Quick Interview Video	149.00	_____
____ Quick Salary Negotiations Video	149.00	_____
____ Why Should I Hire You?	129.00	_____

Dress and Image Videos

____ Looking Sharp: Dressing for Success	99.00	_____
____ Looking Sharp: Grooming for Success	99.00	_____
____ Tips and Techniques to Improve Your Total Image	98.00	_____

Resumes, Applications, and Cover Letter Videos

____ The Complete Job Application	129.00	_____
____ Effective Resumes	79.95	_____
____ Ideal Resume	79.95	_____
____ Quick Cover Letter Video	149.00	_____
____ Quick Resume Video	149.00	_____
____ Resumes, Cover Letters, and Portfolios	98.00	_____
____ Ten Commandments of Resumes	79.95	_____
____ Your Resume	99.00	_____

Assessment and Goal Setting Videos

____ Career Path Interest Inventory	149.00	_____
____ Career S.E.L.F. Assessment	89.00	_____
____ Skills Identification	129.00	_____
____ You DO Have Experience	149.00	_____

Attitude, Motivation, and Empowerment Videos

____ Down But Not Out	129.00	_____
____ Gumby Attitude	69.00	_____
____ Know Yourself	109.95	_____
____ Positive Feet	129.00	_____
____ Take This Job and Love It	79.95	_____

Career Exploration Videos

____ Career Exploration and Planning	98.00	_____
____ Great Jobs Without a College Degree	98.00	_____

Job Search Strategies Videos

____ Tough Times Job Strategies	89.95	_____
____ Very Quick Job Search Video	149.00	_____

SOFTWARE

____ Interview Skills for the Future	199.00	_____
____ Job Browser Pro 1.3	359.00	_____
____ Job Search Skills for the 21st Century	199.00	_____
____ Multimedia Career Center	385.00	_____
____ Multimedia Career Pathway	199.00	_____
____ Multimedia Occupational GOE Assessment Program	449.00	_____
____ Multimedia Personal Development CD-ROM Series	450.00	_____
____ OOH Career Center	349.95	_____
____ School-to-Work Career Center	385.95	_____

SUBTOTAL _____

Virginia residents add 4.5% sales tax _____

POSTAGE/HANDLING ($5 for first product and 8% of SUBTOTAL) _____

8% of SUBTOTAL – – – – – – – – –|_____|

TOTAL ENCLOSED – – – – – –|_____|

SHIP TO:

NAME _____

ADDRESS _____

_____

_____

PAYMENT METHOD:

❑ I enclose check/money order for $ _____ made payable to IMPACT PUBLICATIONS.

❑ Please charge $ _____ to my credit card:

❑ Visa ❑ MasterCard ❑ American Express ❑ Discover

Card # _____ Expiration date: ____/____

Signature _____

Keep in Touch . . .
On the Web!

www.impactpublications.com
www.ishoparoundtheworld.com
www.travel-smarter.com
www.contentfortravel.com
www.winningthejob.com
www.veteransworld.com
www.contentforcareers.com